Navigating Womanhood in Contemporary Botswana

Navigating Womanhood in Contemporary Botswana

Stephanie S. Starling

BLOOMSBURY ACADEMIC
LONDON • NEW YORK • OXFORD • NEW DELHI • SYDNEY

BLOOMSBURY ACADEMIC
Bloomsbury Publishing Plc
50 Bedford Square, London, WC1B 3DP, UK
1385 Broadway, New York, NY 10018, USA
29 Earlsfort Terrace, Dublin 2, Ireland

BLOOMSBURY, BLOOMSBURY ACADEMIC and the Diana logo are trademarks of
Bloomsbury Publishing Plc

First published in Great Britain 2023
Paperback edition published 2025

A catalogue record for this book is available from the British Library.

Library of Congress Cataloging-in-Publication Data
Names: Starling, Stephanie S., author.
Title: Navigating womanhood in contemporary Botswana / Stephanie S Starling.
Description: London; New York: Bloomsbury Academic, 2023. |
Includes bibliographical references and index.
Identifiers: LCCN 2023006093 (print) | LCCN 2023006094 (ebook) |
ISBN 9781350356689 (hardback) | ISBN 9781350356696 (epub) |
ISBN 9781350356702 (pdf) | SBN 9781350356719
Subjects: LCSH: Women–Botswana–Social conditions. | Women–Legal status,
laws, etc.–Botswana.
Classification: LCC HQ1803.S737 2023 (print) | LCC HQ1803 (ebook) |
DDC 305.42096883–dc23/eng/20230214
LC record available at https://lccn.loc.gov/2023006093
LC ebook record available at https://lccn.loc.gov/2023006094

ISBN: HB: 978-1-3503-5668-9
         PB: 978-1-3503-5672-6
       ePDF: 978-1-3503-5670-2
      eBook: 978-1-3503-5669-6

Typeset by Integra Software Services Pvt. Ltd.

To find out more about our authors and books visit www.bloomsbury.com
and sign up for our newsletters.

Contents

Acknowledgements

First and foremost, I wish to honour and celebrate each of the courageous women who trusted me with the intimate details of their lives. Their beliefs and experiences have formed the heart of this book, and I hope my recounting of their stories does them justice. Tumi Sebetlela, my interpreter and guide, helped facilitate many of the conversations that informed this text with empathy and respect.[1]

This research was made possible by the financial support of the Arts and Humanities Research Council, the University of York, and the Government of Botswana, who granted me a permit for my research.

I owe a debt of gratitude to Prof. Claire Chambers, whose keen guidance and optimism kept me motivated. Prof. Gabriele Griffin helped shape this work at the outset, and I'm thankful for her insights. I appreciate the constructive feedback of Prof. Sara Randall, Prof. Stevi Jackson, Dr Clare Bielby, and the anonymous reviewers who provided thoughtful recommendations to improve the manuscript. Olivia Dellow and the team at Bloomsbury Publishing have been a delight to work with.

I am deeply thankful for my dear friends, Dr Nadira Wallace, Dr Patrycja Sosnowska-Buxton, and Dr Robin Burns who cheered me on, provided unending encouragement, offered thoughtful reviews of every chapter, and served as an invaluable sounding board throughout the research and writing process.

I am grateful to Lynda and Jonathan Tosefsky for generously hosting me in their home during my fieldwork, and to Tlotlego Gaogakwe for connecting me with participants and helping with my research permit paperwork.

I am fortunate to work with a team of supportive colleagues who not only recognized how important this project was to me, but made it possible for me to take a month of uninterrupted time to write. Their willingness allowed me the space to create a more thoughtful and comprehensive book.

Finally, I am profoundly grateful for my phenomenal partner and champion, Harry Waine, whose unwavering love, kindness, and support kept me going during the toughest moments of this journey.

Note

1 I have used a pseudonym here on request to protect Tumi's anonymity.

1

'That's how it is here. Men do what they want': Women in Botswana

–Joy

Joy, a confident, smartly dressed woman in her mid-thirties, asks if I have a boyfriend as she trims my hair at her salon in Gaborone, Botswana. 'No', I say, 'I'm quite new around here, I don't know many people'. 'Good', she replies, 'men here have many mistresses. They will give you diseases'. I ask Joy if she has a boyfriend. She tells me yes, she does, and yes, he is unfaithful to her. 'Does that bother you?' I inquire. Joy shrugs and says quietly, 'that's how it is here. Men do what they want.'

Joy's disappointed resignation stuck with me in the days after we spoke, not because her attitude was remarkable but because it was not. Her words epitomized the narrative I had heard repeatedly since I began living in the country – that women endure great disadvantage at the hands of a gender order that favours men, a fact oft acknowledged and lamented by women who nonetheless feel largely disempowered to challenge it. This story felt all too familiar, and I wanted to learn more about the culturally specific manifestation of gendered dynamics in the country I had newly made my home. I decided to ask the women around me about their lives to help me understand what it means to be a woman in Botswana. To this end, I interviewed thirty diverse Batswana women in the south-eastern region.[1] Their stories are the foundation of this book.

Women's role and status

Women in Botswana have historically been perceived as subservient and dependent, subject to male control over their labour, bodies, finances and behaviour (Schapera, 1938).[2] Upon marriage a woman's guardianship was transferred from her father to her husband, and she became her husband's *motlhanka*, meaning 'servant' (Schapera, 1938). Women were responsible for growing and harvesting crops, bearing many children, childcare and homemaking, care of old or sick community members, fulfilling their husbands' sexual needs, and numerous other practical and emotional duties (Schapera, 1938). Despite this weight of responsibility, a woman had little influence and was 'in all respects subservient to [the man's] will' (Schapera, 1938: 151).

While changes in lifestyle and employment patterns have resulted in increased autonomy for many women, they 'continue to negotiate their gender identities against a background of internalized cultural values' (Mookodi, 2004: 127). The socialization of women and girls as inferior is so deeply rooted that recognizing it can be difficult and addressing it even more so (Datta, 2004; Kinsman, 1983). The high value placed on custom disguises the realities of gender discrimination – cultural attitudes have limited the effectiveness of legislative and policy reforms aimed at reducing gender inequality (Government of Botswana, 2000), and the view of women as *motlhanka* persists (Phaladze and Tlou, 2006). My previous research on perceptions of abortion in Botswana provided insight into prevailing ideas about women's rights. An interviewee for that project, Michelle, shared: 'There are some discussions on the radio, the TV, they usually have these discussions. About why women's rights and whatever, it's just making women bigger than they should be. That's what they say. Bigger than they should be, and they're just trying to make women into men' (Smith, 2013: 170).

Today, the picture of women's role and status is complex. Botswana gained independence from the United Kingdom in 1966. It has since remained politically stable with a functional multi-party democracy and has flourished economically, being termed an 'economic miracle' by the World Bank (2010: viii). The discovery of mineral deposits and the careful management of these resources transformed Botswana from one of the world's poorest countries to an upper middle-income nation with a consistently high economic growth rate (Denbow and Thebe, 2006). The administration has reinvested its wealth to the benefit of many of its citizens, with improved education, health, sanitation and infrastructure across the country. The government of Botswana has shown commitment to achieving gender parity at the official level through a litany of instruments and commitments, including: the formation of the Women's Affairs Division and its later upgrade to the Women's Affairs Department, subsequently the Gender Affairs Department; the Policy on Women in Development; the National Gender Programme Framework; the Vision 2016 programme; the Platform for Action following the 1995 Beijing World Conference on Women; the United Nations Convention on the Elimination of All Forms of Discrimination Against Women (CEDAW); the South African Development Community (SADC) Declaration on Gender and Development; the Constitution; the National Policy on Gender and Development; the National Gender-Based Violence Strategy 2015–2020; Botswana Vision 2036; the National Commission and a host of reforms to address gender discrimination in the law (Datta, 2004; Government of Botswana, 1995; UN Women, n.d.).

Assisted by non-governmental organizations (NGOs), the government has achieved some important successes for gender parity. These include equality of access to education, slightly better employment opportunities for women, women's increased political participation and improvements in some aspects of women's healthcare (Bauer, 2011). However, the impact of these developments is uneven, and many women continue to face discrimination and harmful gender norms. Botswana scores 63.8 in the World Bank's 2022 Women, Business and the Law Index, in which a score of 100 indicates gender equality in all areas measured. Botswana's score is well below the world average of 76.5, ranking in the bottom 40 of 178 economies evaluated (World Bank, 2022a). To contextualize the research discussed here, below I give a brief overview of women's status in the law, their access to education and employment, gendered aspects of poverty and key issues in women's health.

Women in the law

Botswana operates a dual legal system in which common law and customary law co-exist. Customary law is a tribal system with variations between tribal groups. It is unwritten and evolves over time, though it is subject to legislative regulation. Common law of the Roman-Dutch tradition describes all other law in the country. The Customary Law Act dictates that customary laws that do not comply with common law are not enforceable, and both systems must comply with the Constitution which prohibits discrimination on grounds of sex (Gender Links, 2022). However, constitutional protection against discrimination is limited – there are numerous areas of law that are exempted, including 'adoption, marriage, divorce, burial, devolution of property on death or other matters of personal law', exemptions that have significant detrimental impact on women. As such, 'equality is formal but not substantive' (Gender Links, 2022). Additionally, Botswana's Constitution does not provide explicitly for women's rights, nor is there provision for protecting women's rights under dual legal systems (Gender Links, 2022).

Though all women formally have access to common law, in practice they more often resort to customary law, particularly for personal disputes; rural women in particular are typically unaware of their rights in common law, geographic restraints prevent them from accessing the common courts and the cost of common law services is prohibitive (Enge, 1985). The NGO *Ditshwanelo* offers paralegal support to people who are marginalized and disempowered in addition to legal education and activism, but like all NGOs its resources are limited. In early 2013 a South African company set up Botswana's first legal aid facility, which offers legal insurance from P100[3] (£6.63) per month (LegalWise, 2022). While this is an important step in making common law more accessible for Batswana women, the lowest monthly cost is still prohibitively high against minimum wages. Personal preference and accessibility issues therefore result in an over-reliance on customary law to rule over family and community disputes. Based on patriarchal values, customary law treats women as minors (Patel, 2013).

The tension between customary and common law was demonstrated in a landmark case, in which a reformist common law judge assisted four sisters in overturning an inheritance ruling set by the customary court. The government challenged the movement of the case into the common law courts, claiming that Botswana was a traditional country that valued its customary legal system (Patel, 2013). However, the court dismissed the government's concerns, declaring that 'any customary law or rule which discriminates in any case against a woman unfairly solely on the basis of her gender would not be in accordance with humanity, morality or natural justice' (Laing, 2012). This ruling was widely received as a positive step in the direction of challenging the discriminatory nature of customary law. Since 2012, the government has been in talks with traditional leaders to discuss how to ensure the protection of women's rights under customary law, and a number of gender committees have been established to this end (The Borgen Project, 2020).

Laws surrounding citizenship have long been a source of inequality between women and men in Botswana. Women's citizenship has largely been recognized only in relation to men, usually their husbands or fathers. Widows were thus made stateless, with potentially catastrophic effects on their economic security (Gender Links, 2022). Legal reforms have sought to widen the scope of citizenship requirements. Unity Dow's landmark challenge to the legality of the 1984 Citizenship Act ensured that the children of a Motswana woman married to a foreign man were eligible for Botswana citizenship (Dow, 2010). More recently in 2022, the High Court of Botswana found that the prohibition of dual citizenship in the Citizenship Act was unconstitutional, following a challenge led by Sithabile Mathe and her family (Citizenship Rights in Africa Initiative, 2022). Despite these significant reforms much progress is required to secure gender equality in citizenship; the Constitution retains discriminatory clauses, such as those related to the citizenship requirements to become President of Botswana (Gender Links, 2022).

Botswana's Constitution does not provide for nor does it preclude women's participation in political decision making, and there are no national quotas for women representatives. Some political parties have internal quotas though these are not met (Gender Links, 2022). Just 11 per cent of members of parliament (MPs) in Botswana are women, and 19 per cent of councillors, a low proportion compared with its neighbours: women constitute 47 per cent of MPs in South Africa,[4] 44 per cent in Namibia and 15 per cent in Zambia, with a global average of 26 per cent (World Bank, 2022). In 2009 CEDAW recommended that the nation take specific action to address gender inequality in political leadership.

Gender-based violence (GBV) is recognized as a major concern by the Government of Botswana, the United Nations and numerous researchers and NGOs, with 67 per cent of women having experienced some form of gender violence in their lifetime, more than double the global average (UNFPA Botswana, n.d.). Though data are yet to be finalized, it is known that the COVID-19 pandemic has caused a surge in incidence of GBV (The Borgen Project, 2020). The 2008 Domestic Violence Act prohibited intimate partner violence (IPV), a subset of GBV, and made provisions for shelter for abused women. However, it is largely considered ineffective in preventing or prosecuting IPV (Ogundipe, 2018).

Barati, an advocate for sex workers who I interviewed for an earlier study in Botswana, shared her experience of the act's effectiveness: '[It is] a very good act that protects women from being beaten by boyfriends, husbands and so on and so forth, but Batswana don't use it, women don't use it. Why? Because it's not disseminated, you know. We [women] still think the law is something that we don't have access to' (Smith, 2013: 170). Customary courts provide an alternative source of legal protection from IPV – cases will typically be reported by the victim's family, and the perpetrator, if found guilty, will be corporeally punished. It is thought unlikely that this system provides any real protection from IPV (Ogundipe, 2018). Bartlett (1994: 2542) notes that 'a gap between a law's reach and the aspirations of those who seek to use it to accomplish substantial societal reform is a common enough phenomenon'. This observation resonates in the Botswana context, where a lag between legislative reform and social change is evident.

A combination of law and cultural practice disadvantages women in matters of marriage and family life, including forced marriage, inheritance, ownership and division of property and assets, and responsibility for children (Gender Links, 2022). Customary law dictates that a man pays *marebana*, a one-off seduction payment, if he impregnates a woman but does not marry her. The payment is negligible, and it is easy for a man to avoid paying it (Brown, 1983). The Affiliation Proceedings Act of 1970 exists to help women secure regular maintenance payments throughout the child's life, but it is seldom used, and payments are not enough to cover the basic needs of a child (Datta, 2011). Bureaucratic delays often mean that women have difficulty getting a court ruling for child maintenance, and enforcing the ruling is problematic when fathers have left the area or refuse to acknowledge paternity. Some women resist taking legal action for fear that the father will use a traditional doctor to place a death curse on the child to avoid maintenance payments (Mooko, 2005).

The 2009 Children's Act requires both parents' names to be included on a child's birth certificate to reduce paternal avoidance of financial responsibility, but its effectiveness is limited, particularly for women who do not wish to state the identity of their child's biological father or do not know it (Mookodi, 2008), or when the pregnancy was a result of rape or incest. The Employment (Amendment) Act of 2010 created new protections for pregnant and post-partum women in formal employment, including a period of maternity leave at a minimum of 50 per cent salary and permission to breastfeed at work for thirty minutes twice a day. However, a woman is only entitled to one maternity leave regardless of the number of children she has (Legal Information Institute, n.d.).

Historically, asset ownership appears to have been distributed between men and women in a complimentary, if unequal system whereby men owned land and women owned crops and structures on land. Kalabamu (2005: 8) argues that these 'customary practices have, however, been unable to accommodate the new order of social, economic, political, demographic, and above all, gender relationships. The pot could not contain the pressure and started cracking'. Attempts to adapt to emerging norms in the context of prevailing customary attitudes led to a lack of clarity around asset rights, which still largely exclude or disadvantage women. For example, the largest share of an inherited estate is usually directed to the eldest son, or in the absence of a male heir, to the father, brother or another male relative.

Though a series of reforms have made it increasingly possible for women to own land, cattle, property and other assets, land ownership and inheritance administration continues to treat women as minors. Government policies typically include no specific protections for women. While recent reforms are somewhat progressive in theory, in practice they 'ignore historically constructed power differences between men and women' and have been ineffective to date (Kalabamu, 2005). However, a promising 2020 amendment to the 2015 Land Policy gave married women whose husbands owned land the right to ownership of their own land. Previously, married women could only own land if their husbands did not, even if their husbands were deceased. The 2020 amendment could be beneficial for women like Tshegofatso Mokibelo, a widow who was denied an application to purchase a residential plot because her late husband had previously owned land, which was claimed by his family after his death (The Borgen Project, 2020).

Education, employment and poverty

The colonial administration neglected education for Batswana; the only available schools were those few established by missionaries and locals, and just 100 people had ever completed secondary school by independence in 1966 (Siphambe, 2000). The government has since made extensive gains in education for both girls and boys. Primary education was made free for all in 1978, and school fees were abolished for secondary schools in 1989 (Siphambe, 2000). At 15.4 per cent of total government expenditure, public spending on education exceeds the 14.1 per cent global average. There are over 1000 schools in Botswana, and a gross primary enrolment ratio of 103 per cent. The gender parity index (GPI) for gross primary enrolment sits at 0.98, which indicates gender equality at the level of enrolment (World Bank, 2022).

However, quality is an ongoing problem for public schools around the country, particularly at the primary level where only 9 per cent of teachers have an undergraduate degree in education, and 0.5 per cent have a postgraduate degree in education (Modimakwane et al., 2015). UNICEF (2020) figures show that around one-third of Batswana children do not have basic literacy skills after four or five years of primary education. One-third of children fail their primary examination, and two-thirds fail their junior certificate. A study of 2500 primary school students conducted in 2017 reported that over 85 per cent were unable to divide and half could not read a simple story, though girls were significantly ahead of boys in both measures (Pansiri and Tsayang, 2017). Quality of teaching and learning practices has been identified as an area for improvement as part of Botswana's *Education for All* programme. While there is room for improvement, access to education in Botswana is exceptional by regional standards. Sub-Saharan Africa experiences the highest out-of-school rates in the world at 61 per cent for girls and 55 per cent for boys (UNESCO, 2016), yet Botswana's lower-secondary completion rate has been higher than the world average for both girls and boys since around 1990, at 94 per cent and 92 per cent, respectively (World Bank, 2022).

Migration for work has shaped much of Botswana's modern history and has affected women in numerous ways. The subsistence agriculture practised by the majority of Batswana has long been unreliable as a result of poor soil conditions and low rainfall, creating the need to migrate for work – first to the mines of South Africa and Zimbabwe, and later to Botswana's own mining sites and emerging urban centres (Motzafi-Haller, 2002). Seventy per cent of Botswana's population were living in urban areas in 2019, up from 17 per cent in 1980 (World Bank, 2022). Women who migrate to urban centres often continue to support their rural families financially, sending money home and returning often to provide hands-on care for relatives.

The responsibility of assisting family members who are geographically dispersed is difficult to manage and causes significant stress for many women (Akinsola and Popovich, 2002). Living outside of customary restrictions on their social interactions, women urban migrants are vulnerable to casual, exploitative relationships that often lead to single motherhood (Mookodi, 2004).[5] Men living in cities have relative freedom from community 'oversight' (Solway, 2016), and as such are often harder to extract child maintenance payments from. The women who remained in rural settlements during Botswana's period of rapid urbanization became increasingly susceptible to poverty as a result of weakening kinship ties (Brown, 1983). Agriculture is historically 'women's work', and most rural women still grow crops today. While women can apply for a land grant, they often lack the resources needed to utilize the land (FAO Gender and Land Rights Database, n.d.); the poverty-reduction effect of the grant scheme is thus limited.

Women's opportunities for employment tend to be low-paid and restricted to the retail, administration, education and domestic sectors; most women in Botswana who earn wages are domestic workers (Phaladze and Tlou, 2006). There is no national minimum wage but rather a series of minimum wages according to sector. The minimum wage for the retail and domestic service sectors, where most women are employed, is set well below a reasonable living wage at P6.31 (£0.42) per hour and P1084 (£72.00) per month, respectively (Government of Botswana, 2021). Women suffer disproportionately from unemployment at 22.6 per cent compared with 19.5 per cent of men in 2020 (World Bank, 2022). Many women are still economically dependent on their partners or male relatives, though such support is unreliable (Mookodi, 2004). The number of people living on less than $1.90 a day has decreased nationally, from 33 per cent in 1993 to 15 per cent in 2015 (World Bank, 2022). However, most of Botswana's poor live in female-headed households (FHHs) (Lekobane, 2015).

As a result of migration patterns, disease, decrease in desire for marriage and other factors, the family structure in Botswana is changing (Dintwat, 2010; Suggs, 1987), with resulting increases in women's exposure to poverty. Polygyny has been unusual in Botswana since independence. Enge (1985) suggests that this might not be in women's interest. Men having several 'mistresses' is culturally acceptable, yet the decline of polygyny has resulted in fewer women achieving the status and economic security of marriage. As such, FHHs are the norm, with 48 per cent of all households being headed by unmarried women (UN, 2019). Evidence of a link between FHHs and poverty had been discovered globally (Lekobane, 2015); and women are exposed to numerous gendered factors that increase their risk of poverty, such as sexual and domestic abuse, caring responsibilities and pregnancy (The Borgen Project, 2019).

Women's health

Botswana spends 6.1 per cent of its GDP on healthcare, slightly above the 5.11 per cent average for the sub-Saharan African region (World Bank, 2022). Healthcare is administered through a decentralized network of clinics and hospitals, some of which are mobile. Health services are largely free to citizens though some require a nominal fee. The family planning programme is incorporated into maternal and child health services (World Bank, 2010), giving women whose husbands do not want them to access family planning the opportunity to see a nurse under the auspices of maternal or child health during or after their pregnancy. The high take-up of these services suggests that they are effective in reducing the numbers of unwanted pregnancies, and the service has been deemed the best in Africa (World Bank, 2010). The Central Statistics Office of Botswana claims that childbirth has become safer for women, with 99.8 per cent of live births taking place in a healthcare facility in 2017 (Statistics Botswana, 2021).

HIV prevalence in Botswana remains among the highest in the world at 21 per cent in 2022 (UNAIDS, 2022), though rates have been steadily declining from a peak of 26.3 per cent in 2000 (World Bank, 2022). Only Eswatini and Lesotho have higher infection rates, at 26.8 per cent and 21.1 per cent, respectively, against a world average of 0.7 per cent (World Bank, 2022). Sixty-four per cent of people infected with HIV in Botswana are women; in 2018, young females aged fifteen to twenty-four were twice as likely to be infected than their male counterparts, and girls aged ten to nineteen are three times as likely to be infected than boys the same age (UNICEF, n.d.). Botswana's HIV/AIDS programmes are widely commended. Anti-retroviral medication is free and accessible and HIV testing is routine in clinical settings. Condoms are available at no cost at clinics around the country, and condom usage is reported at 64 per cent, though this is declining in younger cohorts (Central Statistics Office, 2018; UNICEF, n.d.). There is almost 100 per cent awareness of HIV but detailed knowledge is low (UNICEF, n.d.).

Consistently high infection rates for young women in Botswana despite strong healthcare and preventative programmes have been attributed to early first age of intercourse, gender-based violence, limited negotiating power with sexual partners, forced marriage and condom refusal by men (Akinsola and Popovich, 2002; Langen, 2007; UNICEF, n.d.; Urdang, 2006). Not only are women at higher risk of contracting the virus, but the responsibility of care for those dying from AIDS tends to fall on women too; the time, labour and resources required for the care of the sick are a heavy burden falling disproportionately on women, who are customarily defined as caregivers (Urdang, 2006).

Teenage pregnancy is a serious issue. UNICEF's *All In* initiative has identified teen pregnancy as one of eight priority issues in the country (UNICEF, 2015), and Botswana's Minister of Education and Skills Development, Pelonomi Venson-Moitoi, has expressed concern that 'adolescent pregnancy brings detrimental social and economic consequences for the girl, her family, her community and the nation at large'. Botswana's adolescent fertility rate is relatively low for sub-Saharan Africa at 45.4 live births per 1000 women aged fifteen to nineteen against a regional average of 101 (World Bank, 2022). However, it remains high on a global scale. For example, rates in the United Kingdom and the United States are 12.6 and 19 live births per 1000 women aged fifteen to nineteen, respectively (World Bank, 2022). Contraceptive prevalence is estimated at 67.4 per cent of women aged twelve to forty-nine (CIA, 2022). Yet, young girls are often reluctant to access clinics where contraception is provided for fear of being stigmatized by service providers

(Meekers et al., 2001). In response to this concern the Botswana Family Welfare Association (BOFWA) has set up youth-friendly clinics, however, there are only five of these across the country.

Maternal mortality has decreased from 326 deaths per 100,000 live births in 1990 to 166 per 100,000 in 2019 (USAID, 2015; UN, 2021), but remains unacceptably high for an upper-middle income country. Botswana's Millennium Development Goal (MDG) target of 89 deaths per 100,000 live births by 2015 was not reached, and it is unlikely that the new target of 71 deaths per 100,000 by 2025 will be achieved (UN, 2021). The most common causes of maternal death in the country are haemorrhage, hypertension and complications of abortion, most of which are preventable. Unreliable supply chains, shortage of transport and inaccessible roads all contribute to failure to deliver life-saving care (UN, 2021). Abortion is effectively illegal. The 1991 Penal Code (Amendment) Bill liberalized abortion laws to include the possibility of termination if the pregnancy is a result of rape or incest, if pregnancy endangers the mother's life or if the child would be born with a severe disability. In reality, bureaucratic delays and negative attitudes of healthcare providers prevent the bill from being helpful to women (Mogwe, 1992; Ngwako and Banke-Thomas, 2020). Unsafe abortion procedures are carried out regularly, with devastating health effects.

In the following chapters I explore the implications of women's role and status in contemporary south-eastern Botswana for the lives of Batswana women. My focus is on the construction of womanhood as illustrated through the accounts of thirty women who shared their views and experiences with me. I examine the requirements a woman must meet to achieve full 'womanhood' status in her community. I investigate the costs of womanhood – the burden of expectation placed upon women and the challenges they face in navigating a male-dominated world. Finally, I consider how life has changed for women over time, and how they accommodate and manage the presence of competing value systems in a rapidly changing social and economic environment.

Notes

1   The term 'Batswana' is the plural for people from Botswana and is constructed from the prefix *ba,* meaning 'people of', and 'Tswana', the Bantu-speaking ethnic

group who make up 79 per cent of Botswana's population. Similarly constructed, 'Motswana' is the singular for a person from Botswana, and 'Setswana' refers to the national language of Botswana.

2   I draw on the work of white, South-African born social anthropologist Isaac Schapera for historic context throughout this book. I recognize that utilizing the historical account of a white man to contextualize my own research into Black women's lives may be problematic. Further, Ranger (1983/2015: 262) cautions us to 'free [our]selves from the illusion that the African custom recorded by officials or by many anthropologists is any sort of guide to the African past'. However, I argue that the respectful nature of Schapera's writings and their positive local reception confer a certain legitimacy on his work. His ethnographic writings on the Tswana, the first of which was published in 1938, were contemporaneously unique in that they recognized the people he studied as agents of social change and focused more on the similarities than the differences between African cultures and those of the Global North (La Fontaine, 2003; Thomas, 2009). Schapera was optimistic about women's empowerment and spoke out against Apartheid (La Fontaine, 2003). Progressive for his era, he encountered legal trouble when he published 'sexually explicit' material, and his *Married Life* was suppressed in South Africa as a result (Thomas, 2009). He has been honoured by the people he studied; the University of Botswana presented him with an honorary degree, a street in Botswana's capital is named after him and his work is used in schools and courtrooms today (La Fontaine, 2003).

3   P is the currency abbreviation for *pula*, the basic monetary unit of Botswana. At the time of writing, one *pula* is equivalent to approximately seven British pence (£0.07) or eight US cents ($0.08). *Pula* translates as 'rain', a rare and valued commodity in Southern Africa.

4   In the case of South Africa, the figure is exceptionally high even by global standards. Geisler (2000) posits that women's role in the national resistance against apartheid, and their campaign for recognition during the transition period, earned them uniquely high representation in the new parliament.

5   Throughout this text single motherhood is understood to refer to women raising dependent children without the support of a partner or spouse, and in most cases, without material or emotional contribution from the father of the children.

2

Cross-cultural research: Experiences from the field

Theoretical perspective

Since many of the terms I rely upon in this book are contested, it is necessary to lay out my own understanding and usage of them; and I do so throughout the chapters. At this point, I shall briefly outline what I mean when I refer to *gender*, *women* and *patriarchy*, which are key foundational frameworks of this text. These terms have long and complex histories and have rightfully been subject to many decades of debate. I do not seek to advance those debates here, but to use existing frameworks to support my analyses of womanhood in the contemporary south-eastern Botswana context. I remain mindful that existing frameworks are not fixed; evolving meanings and differences in interpretation across time, space and cultures are inevitable.

When I speak of gender in the context of this book I am referring to a social construct that posits women and men as different, and to a system of practices that organize relations between men and women according to those perceived differences (Connell and Pearse, 2015; Ridgeway, 2011). De Beauvoir (1949/2011: 293) famously writes, 'one is not born, but rather becomes, woman'. She positions 'woman' as a social construct, a situational reality that is formed and maintained through external social and cultural pressures. Butler (1988: 520) theorizes gender identity as a 'performative accomplishment' constructed and maintained through the repetition of acts. She clarifies that such acts are not expressive of a gendered inner self, but actually constitute gender, while promoting the 'social fiction' that gender is an internal reality (Butler, 1988: 528). When I use *women* and *woman* here, I am drawing on a descriptive classification that reflects the conceptualizations of Simone de

Beauvoir, Judith Butler and others – that womanhood and gender itself are social constructs created and reproduced through constitutive acts, removed from biological determinism and gender essentialism.

When I speak of patriarchy I refer to social structures in which men are dominant, the practises of which serve to exploit and oppress women (Walby, 1989). Walby makes the important point that defining concepts in terms of social construction negates biological determinism, and rejects individualism, that is, the notion that every man in a patriarchal structure is an oppressor and every woman oppressed (Walby, 1989). Rather, patriarchy is conceptualized as a system that shapes common norms and behaviours along gender lines in ways that predominantly disadvantage women.

Social constructionism as defined by Friedman lays the foundation of my theoretical approach. Friedman (2006: 182) defines the concept as: 'the theoretical approach of accounting for something by construing its nature and existence as the product, in some sense, of social relationships, practices and discourses'. Social construction theory refutes the idea that universal facts can be discovered and presented by an objective researcher. Rather, knowledge is construed as contextually specific and situational, and its presentation subjective. Social constructionism in qualitative interviewing theorizes the interview process itself as meaning-making, as two individuals (or three, if using an interpreter) together construct an account of the interviewee's experience. The approach makes space for the researcher as an active participant in the research and acknowledges that participants are not containers of pre-existing knowledge from which data can simply be extracted (Holstein and Gubrium, 1995). Social constructionism contributes to the redistribution of power in the research process by laying bare the ever-present influence of the relationship between subject and investigator.

There is an appealing optimism inherent in social constructionism; if entities do not have an independent existence but are merely constructs, then they can be changed through a process of reconstruction (Friedman, 2006; Gergen, 2009). Thus, interviews can be interpreted as part of a wider social discourse and cultural norms and other forces that subjugate women can be transformed through behavioural change (Friedman, 2006). A potential challenge of such an approach is that of conflict arising between the researcher's understanding of the data as social discourse and the participants' understandings of their lived experiences, personal observations and beliefs. However, though the validation of individual accounts may become problematic in the social constructionist context (more on this below), they make an invaluable contribution to research on key feminist concerns in both the empirical and theoretical sense (O'Shaughnessy and Krogman, 2012).

Systemic inequality and misaligned expectations

Human subjects in research are intrinsically vulnerable to exploitation, and this is intensified when the participants are of a lower social, political or economic stratum than the researcher. The more powerful can manipulate the less powerful, even at a subconscious level (Patai, 1991). As a white British woman interviewing Black women from a former British protectorate I was researching within the framework of systemic inequality, putting my subjects at risk of exploitation. Given that I intended this book to highlight the impact of inequality and inequity on women in Botswana, I was particularly concerned that unequal power in the research process might in fact exacerbate inequality for the women I interviewed. Below I give a reflexive account of my positionality and its effect on the research, and of the issues I encountered as a result of assumptions made in the field about my power, status and intention.

Botswana has a relatively nonviolent colonial history. The three ruling chiefs of Botswana requested that the United Kingdom make it a protectorate, and this entreaty was finally accepted in 1885 following multiple appeals. Independence was granted in 1966 without conflict. The colonial period can be characterized as neglectful, but violence and severe exploitation were avoided (Denbow and Thebe, 2006). White settlement during the colonial era was minimal, at fewer than 3000 individuals (Trudgill and Hannah, 2008). There is perceptibly less racial tension in Botswana than in neighbouring countries with devastating colonial pasts, such as Zimbabwe or South Africa. Botswana prides itself on 'peaceful racial harmony' and its lack of ethnic hostility (Makgala, 2004: 11), and was a haven for refugees and activists during the Apartheid era (Makgala and Seabo, 2017). In fact, the black and white stripes of Botswana's national flag represent racial diversity and harmony.[1]

Nonetheless, it would be naive to assume that my whiteness did not contribute to the power imbalance inherent in my research. Though race relations are peaceful in Botswana there remains an ingrained perception of hierarchy, characterized by the view that white people have better access to economic and political resources. Government-sponsored European expatriates received financial rewards for their work in Botswana in the first decades of independence, such as a salary addition of up to 10 per cent and state-funded places for expatriates' children in English-medium schools (Campbell, 2003). Often highly educated, expatriates tended to take on higher-paying senior roles. As such, white people living in Botswana in those years were usually wealthy and privileged (Campbell, 2003), and the perception of white people's disproportionate wealth has lingered beyond the corrective government measures implemented since. Thus, my position of power at the intersection of race and class generated an imbalance that manifested primarily in socioeconomic tension.

When I resided in Botswana it was typically assumed that I was a person of means. I was approached regularly by strangers asking me to hire them or to pay the school fees for their children. In reality, working full time without pay on a long-term volunteer basis and with no assets or savings, I struggled to afford necessities such as transport and medical bills and wasn't in a position to support others financially in any meaningful way. The gap between my actual wealth and others' perception of it meant I was inundated with requests that I was unable to meet, though largely as a result of my own choices. My resources were limited by my independent decision to work unpaid in a country I was unfamiliar with, a choice I was empowered to make by the economic and political privilege of my position as a white, educated, middle-class British woman. In aspiring to meet my felt social responsibilities through long-term volunteering, I was limiting my ability to meet requests for assistance from those with inadequate means and little opportunity to improve their own economic standing. I was presented with an ethical dilemma that was difficult to navigate, and which resurfaced years later when I returned to conduct the fieldwork for this book.

A minority of my participants were middle-class women with well-paid careers, but most were materially poor. Returning to the country as a grant-funded researcher, my own financial status vis-à-vis many of my participants presented an asymmetry that required cautious management. I had more resources than when I had lived in Botswana, and I was financially able to offer support in ways I could not have done previously. However, I was present in a different capacity, and I was wary of the ethical complexities that emerge when social research meets money. Difficulties with subjects of social research expecting gifts and money in exchange for engagement are not uncommon (Ryen, 2003). Conscious of the potential for exploitation of women who might agree to be interviewed only because they needed funds, I chose not to offer payment for taking part. I set this out clearly during the consent gathering stage of recruitment and several prospective participants declined to be interviewed upon learning that it would be unpaid, suggesting that my concern had been legitimate.

Though I did not offer payment in exchange for interviews I was keen to provide some form of compensation for the interviewees' time, particularly to those women who were struggling to meet their basic material needs. Depending on what felt appropriate on each occasion, I brought bags of food and drink to the women's homes, spent money in tuck shops run by their families, or gave gifts to their children. When meeting in cafes I encouraged the participants to order anything they liked on my tab, an offer that was both anticipated and well utilized. While these contributions were materially negligible I believe they served an important purpose; expressing my gratitude for the participants' time and engagement in a way that was immediate and tangible helped to build rapport and to create a feeling of mutual benefit in most cases.

However, on one occasion tension emerged as it became clear that the woman I was interviewing expected considerably more from me. She consistency redirected our discussion to examples of ways women might help other women. She answered my questions briefly, if at all, before moving on to talk about how a woman 'must support her sisters in Africa'. As the interview ended she asked me to act as her legal and financial sponsor for immigration to the United Kingdom with the implication that once her visa was granted, she would move in with me as a live-in employee. The woman had arrived at the interview site in a new sports car, dressed stylishly, with her hair professionally arranged and her nails manicured. My impression of her was of relative affluence, and so I was particularly taken aback by her request and ill-prepared to respond. The conversation was awkward as I tried to explain why I could not employ her. On this occasion it appeared that my race and class identity had given the impression of influence and resources far beyond those I possessed, creating a power imbalance that undermined the interview process and damaged my relationship with the participant.

Ethical stewardship of participant accounts

Participants have negotiating power during the data collection stage, when they can choose whether or not to be interviewed, where and when and for how long, and how cooperative they wish to be during the interview itself (Karnieli-Miller et al., 2009). However, the interviewees' control dissipates at the point of the researcher's analysis and interpretation of the data (Mullings, 1999). It is therefore critical to honour the expertize of the women behind the data through respectful stewardship of their stories, representing what they said with accuracy and care, and acknowledging that the researcher's analysis reflects a single interpretation. I found that this approach produced challenges of representation in instances where accounts had inherent discrepancies, contradicted other sources of information, or where my understanding of their words was 'not only different but potentially threatening and disruptive to the subject's view of the world' (Acker et al., 1983: 428).

There are numerous reasons why participants' accounts might contradict other findings, particularly in non-representative samples like mine. Internal and external discrepancies are to be expected in interviews as like all encounters, each contributor has their own set of conscious and unconscious investments, interests and agendas. My intention was to treat the information shared with me as an authentic form of knowledge in its own right, not requiring external validation through conventional methods of triangulation. In Shostak's (1990) ethnography of the !Kung San women of Botswana she presents full passages from her interviews alongside her own analyses, ensuring transparency and offering the reader the option to draw their own conclusions. Bernick (1991) notes that Shostak assumes no authority in her viewpoints where they differ from those of her subjects. Though the reality of word limits prevents me from sharing fully unabridged passages from my interviews throughout, I follow Shostak's lead in including lengthy sections where appropriate, and in avoiding discounting the participants' views where they conflict with my own analyses. I attempt to treat my participants' accounts respectfully by holding space for narratives that complicate or undermine my own interpretations, and by ensuring that the interview excerpts I choose to present represent as fully as possible what I believe the subject was trying to communicate.

Feminist researchers have critiqued traditional triangulation processes as valuing 'objectivity over subjectivity', an emphasis that is problematic in researching oppressed groups because it undermines individual difference and discounts lived experience (Hesse-Biber, 2012). However, feminist researchers have developed a form of triangulation that allows the researcher to investigate the contradictions within qualitative data without silencing the participants or dismissing their accounts as erroneous or even dishonest (Hesse-Biber, 2012). By exploring the meaning behind inconsistencies, we can open a dialogue between sources in a way that enriches our understanding of the data without diminishing the participants' narratives (Hesse-Biber, 2012). In a study into the widespread practice of male infidelity in Nigeria, Jordan Smith's (2009) analysis of contradictory accounts given by spouses enabled illumination of the social and cultural construction of womanhood, masculinity and family, while holding space for individual agency in storytelling, an approach I seek to follow here.

For example, I had the impression that some of my interviewees were focusing disproportionately on the adversity in their lives. LeVine (1979) notes that in complaining women take on a level of power. By asking interviewees to talk about their lives, the interviewer is positioning themselves as a sounding board, an opportunity that LeVine found her own participants were quick to take. She recalls that women disguised their advantages and represented themselves as victims (LeVine, 1979), a pattern I noticed in my own interviews. This is not to say that my subjects' complaints were exaggerated or lacked legitimacy. Rather, that the interview setting provided a space for women to explore and communicate aspects of their lives they experienced as difficult. Occasionally, this negative bias revealed inconsistencies. For example, many of the women were intensely critical and dismissive of men yet emphasized that they were desperate to find a husband. I followed Jordan Smith's example in using discrepancies to explore broader social and cultural dynamics while preserving the integrity of individual accounts, rather than treating inconsistency as a weakness or falsity of the data.

This reflexive triangulation method allows for comprehensive data analysis while protecting the voices of participants, addressing a power imbalance that favours the researcher at the analysis stage. However, questions remain as to whether white academics of the post-colonial nations can ever truly give voice to postcolonial women.[2] Spivak (1988) cautions that by attempting to 'give voice' to the subaltern, researchers are inevitably presenting subaltern perspectives within the framework of colonial interests, therefore in fact speaking *for* the subaltern. Spivak's critique of research by outsiders in postcolonial locations is difficult to square with the goal of 'bringing women's voices in from the margins' (Ryan-Flood and Gill, 2010: 2), a fundamental facet of emancipatory feminist research, and raises questions about how to write about women from a 'different – implicitly less powerful – social location' (Ryan-Flood and Gill, 2010: 5), without patronizing, causing offence, silencing or exploiting the participants. I do not claim to have solved this longstanding moral dilemma, but I hope that through rigorous reflexivity, transparency of approach and a position of respect towards my interviewees and their accounts, I am offering a meaningful and ethical contribution to our collective understanding of women's lives.

I spoke to thirty remarkable women for this book, all of whom were generous and courageous in sharing their stories with me. There was much diversity among my participants, yet in many cases they shared values, attitudes, and experiences. Together, their words built a picture of greater similarity than difference and informed my own interpretation of the ways womanhood appears to be constructed and navigated. I am mindful that in drawing out the common threads in my interviews I risk essentializing women by treating them as a homogenous entity with a single experience of womanhood. To that end, I pay attention to demographic and experiential differences as I explore and explicate their accounts, noting demographic variables where appropriate. To support the reader in getting to know each participant, basic information on their backgrounds is provided as an appendix for ease of reference.

Insider/outsider and the qualitative interview

In-depth, semi-structured qualitative interviewing provides a fertile and flexible platform for feminist enquiry, offering the opportunity to listen deeply and respond relationally to those whose stories you seek to understand. While structured interviews can reinforce the hierarchal nature of social research by leaving limited space for the subject to direct the conversation (Oakley, 1981), semi-structured interviews allow participants to choose what they want to share within the researcher's area of enquiry, and for women who might otherwise remain unheard to share their accounts on their own terms (Hesse-Biber and Leavy, 2007). Qualitative interviewing prioritizes depth of exploration over scope of responses, making it ideal for investigating the subjective accounts of a small number of individuals (Ambert et al., 1995). Through such methods 'we are able to see different and sometimes contradictory layers of meaning, to bring them into useful dialogue with each other, and to understand more about individual and social change' (Andrews et al., 2008: 1). The practice of storytelling as a traditional tool of meaning-making and cultural reproduction remains commonplace across Botswana (Denbow and Thebe, 2006); a norm that supported my subjects' acceptance of the interview method.

Qualitative interviewing was compatible with my purposes and my research environment. It also offered reward potential for my participants. For the author, the advantage of conducting research is concrete and relatively immediate in terms of career progression and the satisfaction that comes from working within one's field of interest. Benefits of participation for the interviewees are perhaps less clear. However, being heard is often reported by research participants to be a fundamentally validating and meaningful experience (Patai, 1991). According to Finch (2004: 168), her female subjects perceived their interviews as 'a welcome experience' that provided them with an opportunity to discuss themselves in ways that they felt unable to do in their everyday lives. Opie (1992, cited in Scharff, 2010) notes that many interviewees feel empowered by the process. Though a minority of my subjects did not seem invested in sharing their experiences, most seemed energized by their interviews, often thanking me and staying beyond our allotted time to talk about the experience and about whatever was on their minds at the time.

Given the socially dynamic nature of the qualitative interview, my role status in relation to each of my participants was fluid and changeable, subject to the subtleties of interaction present in all social encounters (Holstein and Gubrium, 1995). Being perceived as an insider can improve openness and trust in an interview and contributes to the quality of the interaction and the effective construction of meaning (Mullings, 1999). Having lived and worked in Botswana for sixteen months prior to conducting the fieldwork for this book, I was somewhat familiar with Tswana culture, language and models of social interaction. While this was helpful in building rapport, my level of immersion was insufficient to grant me insider status on the whole. However, as a woman interviewing women about womanhood, my gender identity was a significant shared factor.

In Botswana, as elsewhere, there are topics that are considered inappropriate for discussion between men and women, and a sense of openness and camaraderie can often be found between women even if they do not know one another. I was therefore better placed to conduct meaningful interviews than if I had been male, and I believe my gender identity was crucial to the success of many of my interviews. However, feminist researchers warn against the superficial intimacy created through an assumption of shared experience (Karnieli-Miller et al., 2009; Kvale, 2006; Stacey, 1991), cautioning that this can mask profound inequalities, 'for in a world divided by race, ethnicity, and class, the purported solidarity of female identity is in many ways a fraud' (Patai, 1991: 144). I grappled with my own moral standpoint in this respect, concerned that I might fall foul to unintended or subconscious exploitation of my subjects through an assumption of connectedness. Stacey (1991: 117) points to being 'rigorously self-aware' and acknowledging the partiality of the research as ways in which to address delusions of equality, concluding that the benefits of feminist research outweigh the 'moral costs'.

While my gender and prior experiences of Tswana culture lent me a certain insider status, other aspects of my identity – principally being white, British, an academic and young – marked me as an outsider. My researcher position contributed to my outsider status since observation is intrinsically distancing. As an academic researcher affiliated with a university, my educational attainment was broadly visible and marked me as different from the majority of my participants. I was younger than most of my subjects; twenty-seven of the thirty women I interviewed were older than me. Being unmarried and childfree, I could be perceived as juvenile since marriage and motherhood are viewed as significant life stages for women (Suggs, 1987). Though I was concerned that being considered immature would exclude me from certain areas of discussion, in fact I benefitted from the 'advantages of naïveté' and easier acceptance in terms of the 'investigatory advances of the novice' (Ryen, 2003: 433). Asking participants to describe things that the interviewer is expected to understand can cause confusion or mistrust, and so it was helpful in some cases to be perceived as inexperienced – I was able to ask questions that a woman perceived as 'mature' might be expected to know the answers to already; for example, 'what exactly does childcare involve?'

As an outsider I was perceived as disconnected from certain value systems and taboos. It is possible that research participants might discuss sensitive issues more readily with somebody considered external to the prescribing culture. My outsider status encouraged participants to open up about topics that would usually be off-limits, in particular matters relating to menstruation or sexual experience. For instance, when asking the question, 'when does a girl become a woman?', some interviewees laughed nervously in acknowledgement of the possible connotations with sex or periods. They seemed self-conscious and reluctant to answer, but eventually relaxed once they felt assured that I was not troubled or embarrassed by those topics. While being an insider can be advantageous, it can also blind the researcher to the ordinary and the 'obvious'. Familiarity can cause us to overlook important data (Corbin Dwyer and Buckle, 2009), a pitfall I fell into on more than one occasion when I neglected to follow up on an answer because I assumed I understood the participant's experience. For example, in one instance an interviewee told me she had left school because she fell pregnant. I assumed I knew what this had been like for her and did not give the space to reflect on what her experience had meant to her, which I regretted afterwards.

The nature of my research required me to ask about topics often considered private or delicate. With subjects who were quiet or shy, I felt particularly uncomfortable asking such questions and tended to frame them in a passive or generalized manner or to omit questions altogether. Of course, what constitutes a sensitive subject varies between cultures. I was aware of many local taboos in Botswana because of my previous residence and research there and handled such topics with the appropriate subtlety during my interviews. However, I added topics from my own culture to my 'sensitive' list, not all of which are sensitive in the Botswana context. For example, many participants talked about absentee fathers in a general way, but I often felt uncomfortable asking about their own children's fathers. British etiquette discourages asking questions about non-conventional family structures, particularly where one party has been abused, abandoned or otherwise poorly treated. However, I noticed that my interpreter was comfortable asking questions about absent or abusive fathers, and once I had tentatively explored this area of enquiry myself, realized that my participants were also comfortable discussing the issue. Had I been a cultural insider, I would have been more at ease navigating conversational taboos. Indeed, when interviewing participants from a similar sociocultural and educational background to myself I did not have any problems with asking sensitive questions, and I felt more confident in my ability to negotiate conversational delicacies with women I had more in common with.

In a candid critical reflection on learning to listen, Anderson (Anderson and Jack, 1991: 16–17) shares how one of her interviews was inhibited by 'internalized cultural boundaries' when she failed to encourage her participant to share her own interpretation of events. My English upbringing taught me to avoid impropriety by skirting sensitive topics of conversation. Though I have consciously cast aside this reticence in my ordinary life, it returned amidst concerns around exerting too much influence and abusing power imbalances in the research process and gave rise to self-censorship. Similarly, Anderson (Anderson and Jack, 1991: 13) speaks of being constrained by a fear of 'forcing or manipulating individuals into discussing topics they did not want to'. In my own interviews I often avoided following intriguing lines of enquiry when doing so might have offended the participants or caused them distress, mindful that I had no counselling training nor could I provide resources for support. Though the risk of missing opportunities to give voice to women on the margins by holding back in interviews is legitimate, so is that of causing insult by asking the 'wrong' question.

The balance is delicate and challenging to navigate. Phoenix (2010) describes an incident where she unwittingly caused insult when she asked a white participant whether she experienced racism on account of having a Black baby. To Phoenix, who is Black herself, the baby's appearance was irrefutably Black. However, the participant firmly denied that the infant was Black, cut the interview short, withdrew from the longitudinal study and refused to answer Phoenix's calls. Phoenix suspected that she had challenged the family's narrative surrounding the baby's heritage and caused distress in doing so. Finding the ability to listen amidst ethical concerns, internal boundaries and personal biases was a challenge in my own research. Anderson and Jack (1991) suggest that we can sharpen our attention to story without being intrusive through a 'readiness to be sensitive to the narrator's privacy while, at the same time, offering her the freedom to express her own thoughts and experiences, and listening for how that expression goes beyond prevailing concepts'.

Sample and research site

My inclusion criteria for participation were that subjects self-identified as women and were of Tswana ethnicity. I kept the criteria minimal in the hope of speaking to women with a diverse range of lived experience. However, my sample was not intended to be representative; speaking of slave stories, Bold (2011: 16) emphasizes that while one experience cannot represent an entire group of people, 'many overlapping stories generate a convincing set of evidence to support understanding.' I identified the broadest initial sample possible but did not aim for random selection since this was not required for the type of research I conducted. Multiple factors serve to bias interviewee selection and are inevitable to some extent in most qualitative research. Such factors influencing my sample recruitment include the natural bias inherent in personal networks, the needs for internet access and a certain forwardness to respond to an online advert, and the likelihood I would approach women who appeared confident and approachable over those who seemed shy or standoffish.

I used a variety of methods to recruit participants for my study, including online advertising, snowballing, personal networks and direct approach. Four women were recruited through online advertising. I posted adverts in local community groups on the social networking website Facebook. Drawing on social networking sites can increase the representativeness of a sample by broadening it beyond a researcher's personal contacts (Baltar and Brunet, 2012), and I benefitted from the reach of the platform. Ten of my interviewees were recruited via snowball sampling, a non-probability technique in which the personal networks of existing participants are utilized to recruit further subjects. Snowball sampling is an ideal method for accessing difficult-to-reach groups (Browne, 2005), and for building rapport with interviewees. Even a secondary personal connection with a participant can encourage more effective communication by creating a level of empathy on which subsequent interaction can be based (Ambert et al., 1995). Snowball sampling also encourages trust between the researcher and the researched because both parties can ask questions of mutual acquaintances to dispel any misgivings about the process (Browne, 2005). I recruited thirteen participants using the direct approach, most of whom were from rural areas. This was made possible by the high numbers of unemployed or informally employed women in rural settlements, who are often at home or near home and are not restricted by formal working hours. As such, they were usually available at short or no notice and access was relatively straightforward.

I originally placed age limits on participation, but quickly abandoned my upper limit as I met women keen to share their stories who would have been excluded by my range. Given the practical and ethical complexity of including minors as research subjects, I preserved my original lower limit of eighteen. I remained conscious of the multidimensional significance of age as I recruited each participant. One aim of my research was to investigate how Batswana women talk about their lives in the context of the rapidly changing economic, political, social and material environment that has characterized Botswana since independence in 1966. In light of this, I hoped to hear from women who had lived long enough to be able to reflect on their experience of this shifting environment. I also wanted to include the perspectives of young women and how they differed both from one another and from their elders. Since the qualitative interview is a dynamic form of social interaction not excepted from the relational norms of the setting, it was necessary to assess how my own age compared with that of my interviewees and how that might influence our exchange. Age and maturity have long been significant factors in social interaction in Botswana (Denbow and Thebe, 2006; Schapera, 1938; Suggs, 1987). By and large it is not acceptable for young women to ask personal questions of their elders, a limitation I received rather direct lessons in during my period of residence in Botswana. Requesting interviews with elder women might have been perceived as impertinent, and so I largely avoided approaching women who I estimated to be over fifty.

I interviewed a total of thirty participants. All self-identified as women and were Motswana by birth. All were Black. sixteen resided in rural areas and fourteen in the capital city, Gaborone. The total age range spanned twenty-five to forty-five. Of the sample, five were aged twenty-five to twenty-nine, twelve aged thirty to thirty-four, eight aged thirty-five to thirty-nine and five aged forty to forty-five. Educational attainment varied from junior school level to PhD level: two had junior school education, eight had started or completed secondary school, six had diplomas or certificates, seven had undergraduate degrees and seven had postgraduate degrees. Of the thirty women sampled, seven had no children and twenty-three had children. Of those who had children, five were married and seventeen were unmarried. No participants were married without children. The number of siblings my interviewees had ranged from one to eight. Twenty of the women were employed, seven unemployed, one self-employed and two were students. Of those employed, seven were teachers and three had other roles in educational institutions. Of the remaining ten, jobs ranged widely and included a magistrate, a radiographer, a postmaster, a researcher, a designer, two cashiers, a driver, a customer services assistant and an auditor. Twenty-seven of the thirty participants identified themselves as Christian, one as Muslim, one as atheist and one as agnostic.

I chose south-eastern Botswana as my research site, home of the capital Gaborone as well as rural settlements of various sizes. While the urban areas of Botswana have seen extraordinary change since independence, rural life has remained relatively static (Ingstad, 2004). Rural communities, home to 27.8 per cent of the population (CIA, 2022), have been less influenced by the forces of industrialization and globalization and are a stronghold of Tswana culture. Extreme poverty is largely concentrated in rural areas where employment options are few and far between and farming is rarely profitable (Motzafi-Haller, 2002). Rural-to-urban migration by working-aged women is commonplace; the quick construction of urban centres since independence provided employment opportunities for rural women not available in their home villages. Women moving to towns and cities often leave their children in the care of grandparents back home, distributing the family unit between rural and urban areas (Ingstad, 2004; Motzafi-Haller, 2002). It is common for families to spend large periods of each year away from their primary residence, visiting remote cattle posts or the villages of their kin. Many of my participants were thus able to speak to the prevailing attitudes and behaviours in both rural and urban locations, an area of complexity I examine later in this book.

To ensure that my participants were able to give informed consent to be interviewed, I provided information about myself, my research and what the interviews would involve. I explained how I would use the data, including the potential for publication. I informed them that they could withdraw their participation after the interview, and that they had the right to decline answering any of my questions and to stop the interview at any time. All interviewees signed a consent form, which was made available in writing in both English and Setswana along with all other preliminary information. All prospective subjects were offered the services of an interpreter. To protect the privacy of the participants I anonymized all names and accounts unless requested not to. The research design was approved by the University of York Academic Ethics and Compliance Committee and a research permit was granted by the Government of Botswana.

The limitations of working with an interpreter

Both Setswana and English are official languages of Botswana. Most of my participants were fluent in both languages, though some had limited proficiency in English. However even between comfortably fluent English speakers, Setswana is often used to discuss the cultural and the personal (Bagwasi, 2003). Mindful that failing to work around language barriers can exclude the accounts of the most marginalized, and that speaking in a second language can be tiring and can preclude authentic self-expression (Murray and Wynne, 2001), I offered the option of an interpreter to every participant. Having been unable to source a professional interpreter I hired Tumi, a bilingual Motswana university graduate with prior experience in conducting research interviews. Tumi would play a role in participant recruitment and act as a guide in rural villages that I was unfamiliar with, in addition to interpreting the interviews and translating documents. When engaging Tumi I ascertained that she understood the nature of my research by describing what it was, how I would conduct it and for what purpose. She also saw my research questions, interview schedule, consent form and information sheet in advance of our employment agreement. Tumi expressed her interest in the research and pleasure in my respect for Setswana culture, and I was encouraged by her expression of commitment to the feminist goals of the work.

Although I thought that I had discussed all the relevant issues with Tumi prior to beginning the fieldwork, in hindsight I realized that we had not addressed the question of her level of autonomy in the interviews or precisely how she would translate what was spoken. The independence of her approach in certain interviews came as a surprise to me. Tumi occasionally challenged the participants in their responses; for example, 'but doesn't that contradict what you just said?' My preference was not to confront or lead the interviewees for concern over making them uncomfortable. However, Tumi's pushing often elicited more data as participants went on to explain or clarify their views. It seemed that the discomfort was all my own. Ultimately, Tumi's active engagement helped to build rapport between herself and the interviewee. As Edwards (1998: 204) posits, 'the basis on which we make decisions to pursue or abandon particular issues interviewees raise during interviews is not necessarily more informed than that of the interpreter'. Tumi's proactive input had the positive effect of showing the interviewees that she was invested in what they had to say.

Whether an interpreter ought to speak in the third or first person has been debated (Wallin and Ahlström, 2006). Scholars posit that interpreters must not be excluded from the reflexive turn in social research (Edwards, 1998; Murray and Wynne, 2001; Williamson et al., 2011). Just as the researcher cannot be removed from the research, so the interpreter's own subjectivity and relational role must be acknowledged. Using the third person in translation recognizes (a) the presence of a subjective third person in the interview procedure and (b) that the participant is not able to communicate directly with the researcher (Edwards, 1998). Additionally, many languages cannot be translated verbatim into another language (Murray and Wynne, 2001). Setswana and English stem from different root languages – Niger-Congo and West Germanic, respectively. As such, attempting verbatim interpretation might have skewed the meaning of the dialogue, and it became Tumi's responsibility to prioritize the translation of meaning rather than of specific word use. Allowing her so much control over the process was challenging for me. She would often begin a translation with, 'she is basically saying ... ' when I wanted to know *exactly* what the participant was saying.

The interviews I conducted through an interpreter were less successful and data-rich than those I conducted in English on a one-to-one basis. The former were very short, with answers being brief, superficial and lacking in emotional content. Murray and Wynne (2001) report similar findings and point out that cultural differences could not account for the lack of depth in their interpreter-facilitated interviews, as they did not have the same problem when interviewing one-to-one on the same topic. Williamson et al. (2011) also concede that while their interpreter-facilitated interviews were generally worthwhile, the data they generated were simpler and less nuanced than those conducted without the need for translation. Murray and Wynne (2001) point to a weakness of rapport between the interviewer and the participant that is largely unavoidable when there is no shared language, to explain the relative hollowness of interpreter-facilitated interviews. My own experience supports this; I was unable to build a relationship with the participants I could not converse with directly. Their body language felt distancing, and I got a sense that they were resisting me at some level. Although they willingly consented to being interviewed, they did not seem interested or invested in the process once we began. Where a participant spoke even minimal English this helped us to foster rapport, demonstrating the significance of at least basic shared language in connecting and communicating with others in cross-cultural research.

Misunderstandings can arise when an interviewer fails to phrase a question in a way that is culturally suitable when translated, and abstract concepts do not always translate across a language barrier (Ryen, 2003). In a handful of my interpreter-facilitated interviews with rural women, I was simply not able to get my meaning across, despite my interpreter and I rephrasing and simplifying questions several times. On such occasions we eventually abandoned our line of enquiry and moved on to the next question. This problem appeared to result from a combination of interviewee disinterest and our struggle to phrase the questions in an understandable manner. There were some instances where different participants seemed to misinterpret the same question, which suggested that it had not translated well. For example, 'is there anything else I should know?' received answers to 'do you have any questions?' When translated some questions might appear irrelevant or overly basic to an interviewee. Often when I asked, 'can you describe a typical day?' the participants hesitated and seemed unsure of what I wanted. Phoenix (2010: 90) points out that 'in everyday interaction narratives only become "tellable" if they are new, reportable, unusual, funny, or shared stories', which seemed to be the case in my interviews where confusion arose when I asked about the mundane.

Putsch (1985: 3344) holds, 'a language barrier disarms a communicant's ability to assess meanings, intent, emotions, and reactions'. In conducting the research for this book I came to understand that the advantages of a shared language cannot be overestimated, and I regretted not being fluent in Setswana. While using an interpreter allowed me to grasp the basic meaning of what the participants were saying, I was rarely able get a sense of the feelings behind their responses. Nuances of speech were lost to me. The time delay of translation prevented me from connecting a particular sentence to an accompanying physical reaction, mitigating the possibility of using body language to add depth and emotional context to responses. It is also possible that the participants would have been more willing to disclose their personal experiences and culturally sensitive information to me as an outsider, feeling that they were protected from judgment by their peers. Involving a local interpreter in the interview might have negated this advantage and could explain the high number of reluctant respondents that I had when using an interpreter, a problem that rarely occurred when interviewing without one.

While interpretation during interviews was problematic in numerous ways, Tumi's role as a cultural mediator and guide was invaluable. She was aware of the proper etiquette for approaching people; she knew how to enter a person's yard, how to greet and introduce. The consequences of breaching etiquette became clear during a trip to Ramotswa, when a potential interviewee misinterpreted our intentions and grew angry. Tumi had followed the appropriate formal greeting procedure, asking all the women present how they were, and introducing both of us individually before explaining the research. However, one of the women we were addressing did not hear Tumi give her own name. The woman reprimanded Tumi for what she perceived as an insulting oversight and chased us off the property, an unfortunate misunderstanding with a rather dramatic result. Tumi's assistance in navigating the social delicacies of interacting with strangers was crucial; we were able to avoid any further *faux pas* among the scores of women we encountered.

While I was broadly familiar with the necessary formalities of approaching strangers in village settlements, Tumi had a detailed understanding of nuances that I could easily have overlooked. On one occasion we observed a woman we wished to approach standing in the yard at the back of her house. The yard was enclosed by a short wall, just a couple of feet high. I began to walk around the side of the property to reach the yard, at which point Tumi stopped me. She explained that it would be improper to bypass the house to approach the backyard, and that we would simply have to call out from the front of the house. We did so, but the woman couldn't hear from that position and so we were not able to ask her for an interview. While following social protocol ultimately denied us the chance to hear from this woman, it also prevented an unintentional breach of etiquette and any offence that might have resulted.

Sexual harassment in the field

Sexual harassment and violence are perilous realities for women researchers in the field (Sharp and Kremer, 2006). In investigating the lived experience of women graduate students participating in global health research fieldwork, McAuliffe et al. (2022) found that young women from across disciplines encountered sexual and gender-based violence (SGBV) during research, including harassment, intimidation and assault. The mental and emotional labour involved in attempting to avoid and manage SGBV and its impact places a significant burden on women researchers that is often unacknowledged (McAuliffe et al., 2022). Sexual harassment from men I did not know was relentless throughout the course of my own fieldwork.[3] On public transport or out on the street men would stare intently at me, lick their lips, make kissing or sucking noises, crowd my personal space, follow me, block my path, make lewd gestures, whistle at me and make comments such as 'I love you baby', 'can I have your number?' and 'I want to be your boyfriend'. I was familiar with these forms of sexual harassment from my period of residence in Gaborone, where I'd encountered it at some level most days and had developed strategies to reduce my exposure. Yet, in my role as a visiting academic I was so focused on the quality of my data and on protecting my subjects from harm in line with ethical protocols that I overlooked my own safety. Sharp and Kremer shared similar reflections: in fully inhabiting their identities as professional scholars they neglected to consider that they 'remained female, and therefore open to sexual advances and even violence' (2006: 323).

In the majority of reported incidents of SGBV during fieldwork the perpetrators are men who are directly involved in the research, such as participants and their relatives or colleagues, field assistants, academic supervisors and gatekeepers (McAuliffe et al., 2022; Sharp and Kremer, 2006). By contrast, the difficulties I encountered were exclusively from male bystanders and service providers. Nonetheless, my research was adversely affected. On one occasion I was subject to sexual harassment from bystanders while conducting an interview. A group of young men approached the yard where I sat with my interpreter and one of my subjects, making lecherous physical gestures and sexual comments directed at the *lekgoa* ('the white person'). I asked them to leave and my interpreter repeated my request in Setswana, but they ignored it. The interviewee did not acknowledge the men and continued speaking. It became increasingly difficult to listen to her with my full attention, and I missed some of what she said. I knew that the noise the men were making would jeopardize the digital recording, meaning that sections of the interview would be lost. I became frustrated and distracted, forgetting to ask some of my questions and failing to follow up when I ought to have done. Ultimately the interview was compromised beyond repair.

Knowing that public transport is a high-risk site for SGBV the world over (Gekoski et al., 2017), I contributed additional personal funds to my fieldwork budget to allow me to use private taxis as often as possible. Though I'd personally experienced as many incidents of SGBV from private taxi drivers as on public transport in the United Kingdom and elsewhere, I opted to follow the advice of those around me who discouraged my use of public transport. Heading out on a two-hour taxi drive to a remote village, my male driver at first appeared friendly. He began asking innocent questions which quickly became too personal, such as whether I had a boyfriend and what kind of men I liked. I started feeling uncomfortable and tried to steer the conversation back to neutral ground, but he was persistent. He told me, 'I will put a baby in you'. Nothing further happened, yet I was exhausted by the cognitive strain of managing the situation in the moment and reflecting on it afterwards, and by the hypervigilance and fear I experienced throughout.

The areas where I drew such unwanted attention tended to be locations rarely frequented by white people – combis[4] and bus stops, slum areas and remote roads. I was highly visible as a 'novelty' in such areas. When out in public with male Batswana acquaintances, other local men would interrogate them in Setswana with questions such as 'what is it like to fuck a white vagina?' and 'what does white meat taste like?' Their emphasis on white sexuality suggested a racial element to this behaviour, although I experienced it predominantly as a form of gender denigration, which I attracted partially because I was highly visible as a young white woman. Gina Yannitell Reinhardt reported a similar 'novelty' effect as an American woman conducting research in Brazil, where she was forced to 'fend off comments about her body type and multiple sexual advances' (Ortbals and Rincker, 2009: 289). Peoples (2008) illustrates how structural and economic changes in Cairo, Egypt, such as women moving into the workforce, have undermined male superiority and fostered an increase in street harassment as men attempt to reassert their dominance. Peoples (2008) argues that perpetrators of street harassment in Cairo are typically unemployed men; their socioeconomic status jeopardized, these men wander the streets in groups emphasizing their masculinity to one another by violating women passers-by. Botswana has seen similar structural and economic changes to that of Cairo over recent decades. In the context of increasing financial independence among women and high male unemployment, a crisis of masculinity is being demonstrated by a rapid increase in violence against women (Mookodi, 2004). As a highly visible, autonomous young woman, it may be that I presented a target for the expression of masculine dominance through the vehicle of sexual harassment.

The risk and nature of SGBV in fieldwork is subject to a multitude of factors, including the presence of gendered norms around violence, the power dynamics in operation between key actors and the logistical arrangements in place, to name just a few. Individual researchers employ mental, emotional and practical strategies to avoid and manage harassment and other forms of SGBV, but often lack the necessary support and protection from their institutions in doing so (McAuliffe et al., 2022; Sharp and Kremer, 2006). The crucial and necessary attention afforded to the safeguarding of research participants must be extended to researchers, and ought to include full risk assessments that consider the positional vulnerability of individual researchers in specific fieldwork environments. Budgetary decision making is critical to enhancing safety measures in the field; funding for research must prioritize the costs of protective arrangements. Such arrangements might include carrying out safety assessments, using hire cars in place of public or private transport, ensuring researchers work in pairs or groups, providing site-specific safety awareness training to fieldworkers and ensuring collective responsibility for the safety of all involved. Though a level of risk in fieldwork is unavoidable, it can be mitigated through regulatory processes that take gender-specific risk into account.

Bearing in mind the forgoing research issues, this book attempts to develop an understanding of how 'womanhood' is constructed as a culturally situated social identity among the Tswana in parts of south-eastern Botswana, with particular focus on how women's lived experience is shaped by local expectations of their character and behaviour. While participant accounts revealed significant and sometimes painful levels of constraint and suffering, they also illuminated agency, creativity and quiet self-determination in strategic resistance to gendered norms. In the chapters that follow I seek to draw attention to the accounts of thirty women who generously shared their stories with me, while acknowledging that my analysis of their words is partial, subjective and informed by my own personal narrative, agenda and positional identity.

Notes

1   The black and white stripes are set against a blue background, which symbolizes the rare and life-giving commodities of rain and water.
2   Though my participants and some of the scholars I cite refer to 'West' and 'Western' to represent the richest and most industrialized countries, I use the alternative term 'Global North' to refer to countries that are majority high-income and politically powerful. Its pairing, the 'Global South', broadly encompasses South and Central America, Asia, Africa and Oceania – regions of countries that are 'most (though not all) low-income and often politically or culturally marginalized' (Dados and Connell, 2012). Though I recognize

that no set of terms used to categorize large parts of the world by their socioeconomic and political characteristics can entirely escape criticism, I have elected to use the framework of 'Global North' and 'Global South' for its helpful ability to reference an 'entire history of colonialism, neo-imperialism, and differential economic and social change through which large inequalities in living standards, life expectancy, and access to resources are maintained' (Dados and Connell, 2012).

3   Framing harassment, violence, paternal absenteeism, sexual irresponsibility and other harmful behaviours, particularly among Black men, pose a significant dilemma for researchers (Boonzaier and de la Rey, 2004; Hunter, 2010). Examining these phenomena in a way that is sensitive to social and economic conditions is necessary in a context where racial stereotypes prevail, and yet such an approach might be interpreted as excusing behaviour that has very real life-altering consequences for women, families and communities. I offer no solution to this dilemma in this book, in which many instances of such behaviours are recounted. My approach is to speak to these phenomena from the perspective of my own lived experience and that of the thirty women who shared their stories with me, drawing on related research to situate my findings.

4   Popular but unregulated public transport in the form of small minibuses.

3

'I am now a woman of the nation': Achieving womanhood

–Elizabeth

For women the world over, marriage and motherhood provide a stage for gender-conforming acts that allow their womanhood to be affirmed and rewarded. In the south-eastern Botswana context, as elsewhere, womanhood is constructed as an influential social identity that can in fact only be achieved through marriage, motherhood or ideally, both. This gendered norm appears to be remarkably resilient in the face of national socioeconomic and demographic transformation.

The significance of marriage

Harrison and Montgomery (2001: 39) contend that women in many parts of sub-Saharan Africa have 'tightly controlled roles as biological and social reproducers'. Further, that 'marriage – both as an institution and as a means of sanctioning fertility – confers social status and allows women to meet societal expectations, but does not make them autonomous through fulfilling these roles'. Harrison and Montgomery's findings, based on ethnographic research in rural South Africa, are reflected in my own interviews with Batswana women. Below, I discuss the meaning my participants attributed to *lobola* (bridewealth) and marriage, their lived experience and expectations of marriage and the external pressures they face to get married and stay married. Since same-sex marriage is not legal in Botswana, the term 'marriage' is used throughout this book to refer to a heterosexual union between a man and a woman that is formalized under customary or common law.

In 1938, Schapera characterized marriage in Botswana as a process that conferred legal and social adulthood on both parties. Almost ninety years later, my research indicates that such a view of marriage as a transitional life stage remains prevalent: seventeen of my participants described marriage as a guaranteed route from girlhood to womanhood:[1] 'When you are not married you'll be treated like a girl' (Akhu). This is perhaps unsurprising, for marriage is considered a necessary marker in the transition to adulthood for women in many parts of the world; for example, in China (Gaetano, 2014) and Kenya (Pike et al., 2018). As I mentioned earlier, marriage in Botswana is formalized through the cultural practice of *lobola*. Research in sub-Saharan Africa and elsewhere demonstrates that the payment of bridewealth reinforces gender norms that are harmful to women, such as inequitable marriages, reduced reproductive autonomy, increased intimate partner violence (IPV) and the inability to leave a marriage (Sennott et al., 2021).

However, the payment of bridewealth is also seen to improve relationship stability, demonstrate ideals of intimacy, strengthen familial bonds and confer social status (Sennott et al., 2021). Certainly, the association of *lobola* and marriage with social status was ubiquitous in my interviews, with women of all backgrounds speaking of the dignity and respectability bestowed upon a woman when she becomes a wife. Lesedi remarked that being married would result in her being valued in her community as 'somebody of integrity'. Likewise, Tshepiso explained that upon marriage 'people respect you. You have an image that is appealing to certain people. Unlike when you're not married, you're just another woman. When you have a husband it says a lot about you'. Tshepiso's phrasing implies a perception of unmarried women as unremarkable and suggests there is little possibility of them being considered unique or valuable in their own right. Similarly, Rudwick and Posel conclude in their (2015: 290) study of Zulu women in South Africa that 'from the perspective of the Zulu people [they] interviewed, a female only becomes a "woman" by being *lobola'd* and married'.

Two of the most powerful Christian churches in present-day Botswana – the Catholic Church and the African-initiated Zionist Christian Church (ZCC) – promote marriage as God's will (Denbow and Thebe, 2006). Lenah remarked, 'marriage is something very wonderful created by God', and Mabedi was 'very pro-marriage' because of 'what it says in the Bible, it got so Adam was lonely so [God] brought him a wife'. Tumelo, the only participant in my study who was formally engaged to be married, spoke about her impending union as a divine pursuit, claiming, 'it's important for a woman to get married. God created marriage'. Nonetheless, her account suggested a level of ambivalence about the lived reality of her marital relationship. She anticipated that neither she nor her relationship with her husband would thrive in marriage: 'Marriage, I think, for me, marriage is not going to change anything [...] I know what to expect from him and he knows what to expect from me'. Though I did not ask my interviewees directly about the impact of religion on their view of marriage, these excerpts indicate that further investigation of the relationship between African Christianity, marriage and womanhood is warranted.

Many of the participants in my study placed great emphasis on the meaning and significance of becoming 'Mrs Somebody' (Neo); 'transformed into somebody else, somebody's wife' (Malisa); 'Mrs so-and-so' (Akhu). Sennott et al's (2021: 65) participants shared similar notions, stating, for example, 'the good thing about being married is to be called Mrs., and it helps you have dignity because you have your own husband.' Upon marriage women are granted a newly minted relational identity. Formal association with a man, 'even if it is the crappiest of marriages' (Neo), is a worthwhile endeavour for the life-altering respectability and social standing awarded to married women. Malisa, who was unmarried, believed that through marriage 'you become a different person altogether', gaining a sense of worth that is difficult to achieve through any other means (Hunter, 2010). When I asked Elizabeth if getting married had changed anything for her she proudly stated, 'I am now a woman of the nation'. Marriage served to initiate her as a cultural citizen.

Social and cultural constructions of nationalism, sexuality and gender work together to define and maintain national identity by delineating behavioural norms for women and men (Mayer, 1999). Women 'reproduce nations, biologically, culturally, and symbolically' (Yuval Davis, 1997: 2), primarily by conforming to 'strict cultural codes of what it is to be a "proper woman"' (Yuval Davis, 1997: 47). Elizabeth was consciously contributing to the reproduction of national identity by participating in marriage in its culturally sanctioned form. She spoke of her status as a 'woman of Botswana' with a degree of emotion that was absent when she spoke about her lived experience of being married. When asked about married life she answered only, 'it's okay. It's nice'. The apparent incongruity between Elizabeth's elevated account of becoming a wife and her impassive description of married life speaks to the important separation of the ideal from the reality, which I explore further below.

Womanhood status was available through the vehicle of marriage regardless of age. Basadi shared that at age sixteen 'you can get married, and so that's when you're a woman', and yet older unmarried women are considered juvenile. At age thirty-nine, Tshiamo was disrespected and ridiculed as an unmarried woman in her village, despite having had the same male partner for over twenty years with whom she shared a home. Though they wanted to marry, her partner could not afford the *lobola* payment. Thus, like some of the couples described in Sennott et al.'s (2021) study, they 'remained in state of ambiguity and liminality in their being in a long-term relationship that was not formally recognised due to lack of *lobola*'. Such circumstances are common in communities where chronic unemployment is rife and unaffordable expectations of *lobola* persist (Hunter, 2010). Cohabitation increased from 12 per cent in the 1991 census to 20.71 per cent in 2011, the latest year for which data are available (Central Statistics Office, 2016; Solway, 2016). Cohabitation is not legally recognized in either common or customary law (Mokomane, 2005). If cohabitation is constructed as an alternative to marriage then it poses a theoretical and practical challenge to the institution, significant not least because marriage confers husbands varying degrees of legal and cultural authority over their wives' bodies, labour and finances (Mokomane, 2005). If cohabitation is interpreted as threatening a practice that shapes and reinforces the gendered distribution of power, the community response to Tshiamo's situation could be interpreted as an expression of resistance to cultural change.

Declining marriage rates have been observed in parts of Africa, Asia, Europe, the Americas and Oceania in recent decades. In Botswana 42.9 per cent of women and 47.1 per cent of men reported being married in the 1971 census, while the 2011 census showed only 17.9 per cent of women and 18.9 per cent of men to be married (Solway, 2016). Marriage rates in my sample mirrored national rates; of the thirty women aged twenty-five to forty-five that I interviewed, five (17 per cent) were married – Lenah, Pono, Thato, Tsala and Elizabeth – and one was divorced – Akhu. Theories for the declining marriage rates in Southern Africa are multifaceted and cannot be comprehensively explored here, but a brief overview of some of the key factors posited by researchers in the last few decades includes: women's improved access to education and employment and their resulting financial independence (Garenne et al., 2001); men leaning away from marriage following the decline of polygyny (Brown, 1983; Suggs, 1987); higher numbers of women than men of marriageable age (Brown, 1983); weakening of men's control over women and a more liberal approach to relationships (Izzard, 1985); chronic unemployment (Sennott et al., 2021); the sheer expense of marriage and the inability to pay *lobola* (Hunter, 2010; Solway, 2016); women's perception of marriage as limiting to their autonomy (Hunter, 2009; Mookodi, 2004; Solway, 2016) and women's perception of men as unreliable providers (Hunter, 2010; Solway, 2016).

The attainability and desirability of marriage have been affected by a rapidly changing structural, economic and sociocultural environment. Yet, the majority of the single women in my study wanted to be married, and many venerated marriage as their highest goal. For Reneilwe, it signified the very purpose of her existence as a woman: 'I'm a woman, I can't wait for [being married]. Being married [...] that is the meaning of my life'. Similarly, when I asked Lesedi what she wanted for her life, she said that her only wish was 'to be a married woman'. Overall, it seemed that attainability rather than desirability was the limiting factor on marriage rates within my sample. This finding is reflected in Sennott et al.'s (2021: 56) study of bridewealth in Mpumalanga Province in South Africa, where 'marriage aspirations for Black women are alive and well'. Likewise, Hunter (2010) discovered that most of the women he knew in Maundeni, South Africa, hoped that a man would pay *lobola* and marry them. In both instances attainability, typically limited by affordability, was presented as a more significant restriction on marriage rates than desirability.

Lesedi's story demonstrates how the yearning for marriage is often influenced by the restrictions single women face; a woman's marital status has an impact on whom she may approach to address a sensitive family concern. Lesedi shared her struggle in trying to protect her sister from her brother-in-law's physical and emotional abuse, which she had witnessed over the course of several years. She felt compelled to intervene but was barred from doing so through defined customary channels on account of her unmarried status.

As a married woman she would have been permitted to approach the family for a resolution. Yet, 'as an unmarried woman I'm not supposed to go in those kinds of discussions [...] And if I was married then maybe I will have to go and inform the in-laws to my sister that, "your child is abusing my sister, and I want this to [stop]"'. Since this option was unavailable to her she instead approached her brother-in-law directly: 'But I didn't have that long route, I went straight to him [...] he was like, "How could somebody who is not married come to me?" I said, "I'm coming to you, that one is my sister, and you are abusing [her]"'.

Lesedi's limited social standing as an unmarried woman served to protect her brother-in-law from being held accountable for abusing his wife. Lesedi's account suggests that he was unperturbed by her accusations but was indignant at her circumventing the culturally acceptable pathway to conflict resolution and was therefore unwilling to engage. In cases such as these a woman's marital status can serve to disarm her in her attempts to address conflict, indicating the far-reaching implications of the status-conferring nature of marriage. Lesedi anticipated that if she were to marry she might be faced with the same struggles as her sister. Yet, knowing 'how to handle all those issues', she actively sought marriage for the influence and respectability it would bring her.

The realities of married life

While most of the women I interviewed held the institution of marriage in high regard, their expectations of the marital relationship were pessimistic. Unreliable behaviour, infidelity and violence on the part of men were largely considered unavoidable. Research suggests that companionate or romantic marriage has gained appeal in many African countries where unions 'rooted in complementary spheres of action' have historically been construed as the regional norm (Thomas and Cole, 2009). By contrast, many of my participants gave the impression that emotional support, sexual attraction, affectionate love and other aspects of a companionate marriage did not form part of their expectations of the marital relationship; the reputational benefit of being married was the primary appeal, and in some cases, the sole appeal. That is not to suggest that the women I interviewed had no desire for intimacy in their relationships; the enhanced reputation they sought was achievable only through marriage, whereas marriage was not a requirement for emotional and sexual connection. Rather, women's desire for good standing in their community took priority over their romantic aspirations when it came to marriage. In a similar vein, Jordan Smith's (2009: 174) study of Igbo women's strategies for dealing with their husbands' infidelities found that, even in love unions, 'after marriage the duties of being a wife and mother subsumed most of their time and effort and interfered with and often eclipsed any attempts to make spousal intimacy a central feature of married life. Some women lamented these changes, but most saw the duties of being a wife and mother as inevitable'.

Women commonly report that upon becoming a wife they are subjected to gendered expectations that were absent from the courtship phase of their relationship, suddenly feeling obligated into subservience to their new husband and his family (Denbow and Thebe, 2006; Harrison and Montgomery, 2001; Jordan Smith, 2009). The women I interviewed reported a similar experience. For some the transition in their role was anticipated, for others it came as an unwelcome surprise. The shift in relationship power dynamics holds particular challenges for highly educated women and those with successful careers, who tend to be accustomed to a level of autonomy. Shera described the experience of a 'brilliant' friend, who had recently married a 'brilliant' and 'progressive' man. Recounting the difficulties that her friend had been bewildered to face since her recent wedding, she explained: 'There's just this constant barrage of a reminder that "you are a wife, you are a woman"'. Before the couple wed they shared an equal partnership, which changed immediately upon marriage: 'when you were still dating it didn't mean that [you were submissive]. You weren't a woman, and now you are a woman, you are a wife. And somehow there comes all these things that nobody sort of told you'. Now a 'wife', this accomplished career woman was under pressure from her husband, his friends and his friends' wives to serve and submit to her new spouse. Her story speaks to the transformative power of marriage in gender relations, which can draw conservative values into otherwise progressive relationships. For women and men entering marriage, 'along with their new status comes new codes of behaviour' (Denbow and Thebe, 2006: 152). Sennott et al. (2021: 63) reported a similar phenonium in rural South Africa; one of their participants declared that 'in marriage you will be treated as a domestic worker'.

Keatlaretse was the only participant who correlated marriage with companionate ideals, describing a 'proper family' as 'two people who love and take care of each other' raising children together in a 'stable home'. Keatlaretse's optimistic aspirations for marriage were at odds with her rather distressing relationship experiences, which will be explored later in this chapter. Additionally, her own father abandoned his wife and children to marry someone else and disappeared from Keatlaretse's life altogether. As an adult she discovered that the woman her father was married to did not know Keatlaretse existed. Having longed for a relationship with her father, she was incensed to find out that he had not acknowledged her existence to his new family. She wanted to approach her unknowing stepmother, but her brother and uncle implored her not to on the grounds that a marriage would be ruined. For Keatlaretse's family, her father's marriage took priority over her need to reconnect with him. Relatively powerless in family disputes as a single woman, Keatlaretse felt she had no choice but to stay silent.

Women in Botswana are frequently abused physically, sexually, emotionally and economically within marriage and relationships, both historically and contemporaneously (Government of Botswana, 2019; Maundeni, 2002; Mookodi, 2004; Phorano et al., 2005; Schapera, 1938). In 1938 (158), Schapera wrote, 'wife beating is common and is considered quite justifiable if the woman is unfaithful, stays out at night, or neglects any of her ordinary domestic duties'. Little seems to have changed in this regard since Schapera's time and IPV against women remains a major cause of concern. The 2018 Botswana National Relationship Study revealed that 37 per cent of women have experienced some form of IPV, and 17 per cent of men admit to perpetrating such violence (Government of Botswana, 2019). By comparison, the average for sub-Saharan Africa is 33 per cent, and the global average is 27 per cent (Sardinha et al., 2022).[2] The most common form of IPV reported in the National Relationship Study was emotional – which might include enforced deprivation, verbal abuse and demeaning or insulting comments – followed by physical, economic and sexual violence in order of prevalence. Eighteen of my interviewees said that abuse within intimate relationships was among the most significant and widespread problems facing women and girls: 'Most of the time you will hear [the] husband is beating up women, [the] wife is being raped, you see' (Reneilwe). Descriptions of IPV included physical, sexual and psychological abuse, as well as controlling behaviours such as limiting access to resources. Some of my participants had been abused themselves, others had close female friends or family members who had experienced IPV.

For disempowered women who do not have access to education or employment, dependent relationships with men are often their only option for survival. Sefela perceived that women are vulnerable to abuse because poverty makes them 'desperate', willing to attach themselves to sexually and physically violent men 'who could either abuse her physically, or even infect her with [sexually transmitted] diseases' through marital rape. Elizabeth also spoke of marital rape, explaining that 'when [she] does not want to be having sex, he just says "no, let's have sex"'. Laone shared that 'there is a lot of abuse, women are forced to do things they don't want to do', implying sexual coercion within marriage. Emelda, Lenah and Kesegotfetse also voiced the view that women of low socioeconomic standing are at greater risk of IPV, including marital rape – each suggested that increasing economic uncertainty was leading women to enter abusive and exploitative relationships with men who could provide financial rewards, 'because some of them, they are not financially capable to live alone' (Kesegofetse). Indeed, dependent marriages are known to be common in Botswana because of high unemployment rates among women, whose dependency makes them vulnerable to sexual violence and other forms of IPV (Mookodi, 2004). Phorano et al. (2005) report that the practice of *lobola* is often misunderstood as meaning the husband has paid for total physical rights to his wife, thus facilitating sexual violence within marriage. Marital rape is not acknowledged by either common or customary law in Botswana, further enabling sexual violence within marriage by implicitly offering impunity to the perpetrator (Swartz et al., 2015).

Conversely, women who are financially independent are also at risk of abuse if their partners perceive their success as a threat to their masculine authority (Mookodi, 2004). Since the 1970s, women have had access to formal employment and increased educational opportunities in Botswana. Thus, they are finding status in areas previously dominated by men, a transition often perceived as threatening to men's established roles as breadwinners and decision makers (Mookodi, 2004). Simultaneously, men are suffering from high rates of unemployment: 19.5 per cent in 2020 (World Bank, 2022). As men struggle to adjust to shifting gender identities, IPV functions as a means of re-establishing their authority in the household (Mookodi, 2004). Some of my participants had recognized this trend; Taemane attributed abuse to 'the fact that woman are now working [...] he thinks you've got a better job. Or he wants you to do certain chores at home because he undermines your job'. Keatlaretse described a marriage within her family, in which a husband was abusing his wife because he could not bear that she earned more money than him.

Silberschmidt (2001) reports a comparable phenomenon in Kenya, a country that has experienced similar socioeconomic change to that of Botswana. In the pre-colonial era, gender roles were clearly defined; women produced food while men fought, herded cattle and engaged in politics. When the colonial government introduced taxation men migrated to urban areas to earn cash to pay their taxes, establishing a new role as breadwinners. Following the Second World War mass unskilled labour was replaced with smaller numbers of skilled workers. Compounded by population increase, male unemployment grew and women took on their own enterprises, shifting the economic balance of power within the household onto more equal footing. As a result, large proportions of men have become frustrated and report feeling 'destitute', 'resorting to aggressive and violent behaviour to assert their authority' Silberschmidt (2001: 664).

The notion that male economic fragility threatens masculinity and provokes IPV is widely substantiated in the African context. In the 2012 Botswana Gender Violence Indicators Study, women who were educated and employed reported higher prevalence of IPV than those who were unemployed and had less education (Ogundipe et al., 2018).[3] Research based on focus groups or interviews with male IPV perpetrators in Ghana (Baffour Adjei, 2016) and South Africa (Boonzaier and de la Rey, 2004; Mathews, Jewkes and Abrahams, 2015; van Niekerk and Boonzaier, 2015; van Niekerk and Boonzaier, 2016) further support the view that self-perceived failure in the performance of manhood is a common factor in acts of violence against wives and partners. Perpetrators frequently describe a gendered sense of powerlessness when lack of access to secure employment leaves them unable to fulfil the role of provider, a cornerstone of the masculinity they seek to inhabit. Acts of violence in general, and of IPV in particular, are constructed as a highly visible and culturally acceptable restoration of masculine control and authority (Mathews, Jewkes and Abrahams, 2015).

Research based on interviews with incarcerated men in South Africa who had murdered their partners highlights the potential for an extreme violent response to underemployment – of the twenty men in the study, three committed intimate partner homicide (IPH) within a year of losing their job (Mathews, Jewkes and Abrahams, 2015). In Botswana, cases of IPH perpetrated by an intimate partner or spouse are known locally as 'passion killings'. Victims of IPH can be any gender, though women were the victims in 92 per cent of the cases recorded by the Botswana Police Service between 2003 and 2012. In the first nine months of 2018, eighty-seven women were murdered by their partners (Bagai and Faimau, 2021). Pamela spoke about IPH during her interview, describing her fear that should she attempt to leave an abusive relationship in the future she was at risk of being killed by her partner. She explained: 'You know like [women are] abused. And they say, "You know what, I don't want to be with you anymore because you abuse me, you beat me up." That happens a lot. Like, when the girl doesn't want the relationship anymore. The passion killing is like that.'

An analysis of the representation of female victims of IPH in the Botswana print media between 2010 and 2013 concluded that victim blaming is pervasive, with articles tending to focus on the female victim's behaviour leading up to the killing, rather than on the act of murder itself. The authors argue that such representation of women who are killed by their intimate partners or spouses 'reinforces, perpetuates and naturalises a vicious gender circle' (Bagai and Faimau, 2021). A culture of victim blaming can be a powerful contributor to self-blame in victims of IPV, preventing them from seeking support. When I asked Pono, who experienced IPV, what she thinks stops women from asking for help, she answered: 'You feel embarrassed. You feel like it's your fault that you are going through that.' Self-blame among women survivors of IPV is of course not unique to Botswana. Self-blame is referenced in studies of IPV in diverse populations globally (e.g., see Babcock Fenerci and Deprince, 2012; Cotter and Savage, 2019; Eckstein, 2011; Greene et al., 2019; Ibala et al., 2021; Mahamid et al., 2022; O'Neill and Kerig, 2000; Reich et al., 2014).

Keatlaretse shared that the father of her child was emotionally abusive towards her, yet she was unable to leave the relationship without her family's sanction: ' … and right now I'm waiting for my parents to act. I've told them my situation and I'm just sitting here. I don't know what is going on'. Her options for acting to protect herself were limited by a cultural norm that dictates conflict resolution within marriages or long-term relationships where children are involved must be directed by elders and kept within the family: 'If I want to end this relationship I can't just do it between me and him, because we have a child. It will have to go through my parents as well, and also through his parents'. The influence of parents is a significant factor in keeping women in abusive or unhappy marriages or serious relationships; girls are taught to be passive and obedient, and their parents often encourage them to persevere (Maundeni, 2002). Pono shared that 'sometimes, you know, there are other elders that will poorly advise, "When you are married, let the things that happen in your house remain there, don't tell people what's going on", and sometimes I guess that's what makes people stay in abusive relationships or abusive marriages'. Speaking of the abuse her sister faced, Lesedi reported a similar problem: 'In our culture, they try to, let's say, be secretive. She will be abused, she will go to the in-laws and tell them, and then they will say, "Yeah yeah yeah, we will just tell him [to stop]"'. Lenah explained that a woman complaining openly about a dysfunctional or abusive marriage would risk being judged as a lesser woman, a fear that prevents her from seeking help: 'You'll be staying home when your husband drinks, there is no food for your children, there is little, there isn't a place to get help from because culturally you know you can't go around saying, "My man is beating me", [they will say], "What kind of a woman are you?"' Marriage for women is thus perceived as a site of devotion to others, of abrogation of the self. While marriage affords status, it restricts women's opportunities for autonomy and self-preservation.

Seven of the participants in my study expressed serious concern around the sexual abuse of girl children perpetrated by their own existing or potential husbands, as well as by fathers, stepfathers, uncles and other male family members. Reliable data on the prevalence of child sexual abuse (CSA) is limited globally, including in Botswana (Ramabu, 2020). However, it is known to be a 'major problem' (UNICEF, 2019). Eighty-eight per cent of the women who reported having experienced IPV in the 2012 Botswana Gender Violence

Indicators Study had been abused as children, as had approximately two-thirds of self-admitted male perpetrators (Ogundipe et al., 2018). In 2018 UNICEF and the Government of Botswana jointly launched the *E Seng Mo Ngwaneng* ('Touch Not the Child') campaign to sensitize the population to CSA and encourage collective accountability for child safeguarding against sexual abuse (Ramabu, 2020; UNICEF, 2019). Tumelo told me that her mother's brother was caught molesting his infant niece, who was later discovered to have contracted HIV. When I asked her how this was dealt with, she said, 'it's an issue that is just kept in the family' and asserted that 'Batswana in general [...] we face a lot of this statutory rape, there will be incest'. While it is possible that she sought to normalize her uncle's behaviour by claiming CSA is common, other interviews supported the view that it happens often.

Keatlaretse was raising her sister's two young daughters along with her own son at the time of our interview:

> I have these two girls, and I have brothers who drink and all that. I still feel uncomfortable when I'm not around, [wondering] if they are safe. We are at a point where you are even afraid of the uncles if they are with the girls. I mean when I was growing up, it was okay for my uncle to bath me and all that. But now, I don't feel comfortable with them doing that, you know.

Keatlaretse expressed similar fears in relation to a potential future husband, acknowledging that a propensity for CSA was something she would be wary of in men she dated: 'if for instance they were my kids and I get married to somebody who is not their father, the fear of him not being a good father to them, the fear of him maybe wanting to do certain things to them'. It was striking that some of my participants considered CSA to be so commonplace that they factored it in as a risk in their evaluation of men for marriage. Maatla, the mother of a teenage girl, was hesitant to marry out of concern that 'the man then ends up making the child his woman as well. Having intercourse, or maybe even abusing the child behind [the mother's] back'. Tsala, who was married, lived in fear of her 'girl child being abused by the father, sexually abused'. The participants who raised the issue of familial CSA framed it as a somewhat inevitable part of married life.

As with violence and other forms of abuse, chronic male infidelity was portrayed as an unavoidable aspect of marriage by many of the women

I interviewed: 'most women have gone through it' (Mabedi), or as Emelda put it, 'cheating is [men's] hobby'. Infidelity in men has long been culturally sanctioned, reinforced by proverbs such as: 'a man, like a bull, cannot be confined in a kraal' (Schapera, 1938), 'a man, like an axe, must be shared' *(monna selepe wa adimanwa)* and 'a man is like a melon seed that spreads around' *(monna thotse wa nama)* (Molosiwa, 2016). These phrases suggest that male libido is an untameable natural force that cannot be controlled by one woman alone. Similarly in Nigeria, the term 'man no be wood' is employed to claim that, unlike wood, men have strong sexual urges that can only be satisfied by sex with multiple women (Jordan Smith, 2009).

The notion that men cannot control their sexual urges is persistent in cultures outside of sub-Saharan Africa, too (e.g., see Christoforou, 2018), and is universally harmful to women who are expected to accept, and even support such expressions of hegemonic masculinity. In Botswana, polygyny was prevalent in the pre-colonial era but decreased during British rule and was ultimately made illegal under common law (though it is still infrequently practised under customary law). Yet, the gendered belief that men require multiple concurrent sexual partners has persevered (Upton and Myers Dolan, 2011). In fact, Neo claimed, 'if a man does not cheat on his wife or whatever, he's seen as abnormal'. Conversely, in Botswana, Nigeria and elsewhere, married women may not have relations with any man other than their husbands, and even single women are expected to remain relatively chaste (Jordan Smith, 2009; Rapoo, 2013; Upton and Myers Dolan, 2011). The prevailing 'notion that men naturally want or need multiple sexual partners is reinforced by gendered norms that perpetuate a double standard about extramarital sex' (Jordan Smith, 2009: 167).

Some of the participants reported that they or their friends had experienced partner infidelity, but although they were unhappy about it, they did not leave the relationship. Shera told the story of a close friend who had discovered that her partner of over ten years had a two-year-old child with another woman. Despite being distraught over his infidelity and concealment, 'she was begging him' to marry her and did go through with their wedding. Being married was, for her, a greater priority than finding a spouse who would meet her need for trust and exclusivity. Basadi described a friend's similar experience: she had confronted her partner upon discovering he was unfaithful, but eventually accepted his promiscuous behaviour and stayed in the relationship despite the emotional distress his behaviour caused her: 'She accepts it, you know she, at this point knows that he cheats, knows that he's done it multiple times, and has no real intention of stopping. He barely apologized. You know what I mean. His apology was sort of, "Well, this is who I am, either deal with it or don't". The man's reaction to being accused of infidelity illustrates his expectation of impunity in the matter, a belief that ultimately proved valid when he faced no consequences. Researchers in other sub-Saharan African countries have also reported that women are aware of their husbands' and partners' infidelity yet rarely seek to challenge it (Cole, 2009; Jordan Smith, 2009), suggesting a region-wide cultural reality.

Khana's interview further supported the view that men who are promiscuous in relationships are immune to the consequences of their behaviour, which could be fatal for their wives and other sexual partners: 'Imagine the man is fooling around, running around. Sometimes he's going to take HIV from me and come to give it to the wife. And the wife can't say anything. She is just going to wait for her death.' Botswana has the third highest HIV prevalence rate in the world, at 21 per cent (UNAIDS, 2022). It is widely considered that most HIV-positive women in Africa are infected by their spouses or partners, who are usually thought to have contracted it through casual sex with other women (Jordan Smith, 2009). I asked Khana to elaborate on why 'the wife can't say anything', and she spoke about the violent response she would expect from her latest partner if she challenged his behaviour: 'Even if he's gone for two days, it's so hard for me to ask him where he was. [...] You are not supposed to ask the man this. The men here in Botswana they know they [can] hurt you. [...] you are supposed to accept it.'

The Setswana proverb 'no woman must dare question her husband's movements' ('*monna ga a botswe gore o tswa kae*') indicates an attitude that is culturally embedded (Molosiwa, 2016). Taemane was of also the view that women who challenge their husband's extramarital sex are likely to be subject to a violent response. Lesedi shared that her sister faced aggression from her husband when she complained about his affairs with other women. Since women are instructed not to address their husbands' infidelity, it can be difficult for them to gain the support of their families should they experience IPV as a result of doing so (Denbow and Thebe, 2006; Jordan Smith, 2009).

Likewise, in Nigeria women are prevented by custom from asking their husbands or partners about their sexual behaviour outside of the relationship (Jordan Smith, 2009). With cultural sanctions preventing women from questioning their partner's whereabouts or asking who he has been with, men are potentially more likely to engage in risk-taking sexual behaviour since they are unlikely to be held accountable.

Most of the women in my study spoke disparagingly of men who were unfaithful to their partners or wives and were frustrated by their behaviour. Others were more accepting. Keatlaretse spoke about a previous boyfriend who she had been content with, describing him as a 'good guy', a 'nice guy', despite having known all along that 'he had a girlfriend' outside of their relationship. She did not view his disloyalty as a negative personal trait nor as unacceptable behaviour. Rather, she saw his multiple relationships as simply an inevitable situational reality. Other women directed the blame for male infidelity inwards. Akhu blamed herself for not being present to fulfil her husband's sexual needs during a period when she studied abroad, qualifying her husband's infidelity with 'men will not just sit alone and wait'. She held herself accountable for her husband's extramarital affairs and the resulting breakdown of their marriage. Mpho also commented on the perception that male infidelity was usually women's fault:

> Women are made to feel that, you know you can't ask about it. You can't say anything. He's providing for you. […] [women will] go home and try to talk to their mothers, and you know their mothers are even just like, 'you need to go back, and you need to, you know, either fix it, or', you know somehow it's still the woman's fault that her man is going out and cheating on her. You know it's either, 'oh it's because I told you, you work so many hours, so you know, what else do you expect?' or, 'you refuse to cook, the helper does it all the time', so he doesn't know what a real woman is because you're not cooking at home. So it's, it's always things that, it's the woman's fault.

In Nigeria too, women are blamed for their husband's infidelity, often by other women. Wives are 'complicit in enabling men's extramarital sexual behaviour' by concealing their husbands' affairs; since their perceived success as wives would be undermined by knowledge of a cheating husband, it is socially pragmatic to cover up their husband's indiscretions (Jordan Smith, 2009: 171–9).

Some of my interviewees not only sought to conceal their partner's infidelity from the community but from themselves, going out of their way to avoid confirming their ongoing suspicions. Mabedi asserted that male infidelity is 'in their DNA […] men can't help it'. She was confident that her partner, whom she expected to marry soon, was having sex with other women and would continue to do so once they were married. Deeming it inevitable, she employed strategies to avoid and manage the emotional distress that evidence of his affairs would cause her: 'I always tell my boyfriend, "Just be semi-ly faithful as you are, and we are good." You know what semi-ly is? Semi-ly is that according to me you are faithful, I don't know what other people know […] I don't really know what he does when I'm not there. So it's sort of if I never find out it's good.' As long as her partner kept his transgressions to himself and continued to behave well in her presence, she would not complain. Her view echoes Schapera's (1938: 156) finding that 'if the husband is unfaithful to his wife, she appears in general to be fairly complaisant about it'. Speaking of Nigerian women who remain in their marriages in the face of their husbands' adultery, Jordan Smith (2009: 173) posits that their decision to stay 'is powerful testimony to the importance of wifehood and motherhood as social identities'. My interviews suggest that such an interpretation applies in Botswana, where the social status conferred on married women would be too great an advantage to sacrifice by leaving a marriage on grounds of infidelity.

In 1940 (189), Schapera said:

If I appear to have stressed the unhappy marriages too much, and to have paid little attention to the happy ones that do also exist, it is because the latter, as far as I could judge, are comparatively rare […] almost always there were complaints of sexual ill-treatment or of infidelity, and the characteristic female attitude was one of resignation rather than happiness.

Sennott et al.'s 2021 (63) study reflected similar findings; one of their participants stated, 'married women are suffering […] we [women] accept everything that men bring to us. All we want is to build a family'. Collectively, my interviews supported this discouraging view of the realities of marriage, epitomised by Khana's declaration that in marriage, 'there is no woman who is not crying'.

Pressure to marry and stay married

Coercion around marriage is prevalent globally; emotional, cultural, religious, economic and physical forces affect women's agency in 'myriad ways [...] whatever their culture, ethnicity, religion or class' (Anita and Gill, 2009: 168). Several of my interviewees spoke of carrying the burden of familial and community expectations to get married, whether or not they desired it for themselves (though, most did wish to get married at some point). Pono recalled feeling the pressure to marry from a young age: 'If that doesn't happen, the society looks at you as if you are now a failure [...] and sometimes it's a bit discouraging, the insults that you get from the elders.' Speaking of her aunts, Shera, who had a boyfriend, similarly complained, 'everybody is [saying], "Where's the husband? [...] Why isn't he marrying you?"'. Their phrasing is noteworthy, in that it simultaneously places the blame for remaining unmarried on Shera while locating the decision-making power with her boyfriend. Such a view serves as both a critique of individual character and a rejection of the possibility of women's agency in remaining unmarried.

Emelda was also judged harshly by married women for being unmarried: 'If you are getting older and you're not married they think that you are stupid or something. Some of them think that you are very stupid, that you better get married. Maybe you are a bully or maybe you are something else, you are not married.' Likewise, Kesegofetse, a passionate and ambitious magistrate who had chosen to marry only once her career was established, realized that her colleagues thought there was 'something she [was] doing wrong to men'. The gendered female figure of the 'spinster', used in many English-speaking countries to identify and denigrate women who remain single in their advancing years, is also to be found in Botswana. Broadly equivalent to spinster, the derogatory Setswana term *mafetwa* translates as 'those who have been passed by'. The gendered trope in which unwed women who have passed 'marriageable age' are villainized as reclusive and undesirable is globally pervasive, and dozens of languages have words for spinsters. For example, *uzendazamshiya* in Zulu (Hunter, 2010), *shengnü* in Chinese (Gaetano, 2014), *bayra* in Moroccan, *solterona* in Spanish and *alte Jungfer* in German. Movements to shift the narrative around older unmarried women are gaining traction in some parts of the world (see, for example, John, 2022), but the sexist trope is generally resilient.

Mpho felt significant pressure to marry from her mother and this put a strain on their relationship: 'I feel like a lot of things my mom says to me and comments she makes that make me upset are about marriage. You know, they're about how I should act as a woman, which means you know, basically marriage.' Mpho was highly educated, socially popular, well-travelled, ran her own home and was employed full-time in a stable job that she was very good at. She was also single. Though Mpho's mother was supportive of her achievements, they were in areas considered external to the cultural pursuit of womanhood and were not deemed a sufficient substitute for the identity-defining accomplishment of marriage. Mpho elaborated: 'As you get older you're supposed to exhibit this person, this woman, you're supposed to be showing that you're a woman who is there for marriage [...] there's a certain age where women just become marriage material.' Neo also struggled with pressure from her mother to prioritize marriage and marital childbearing, which increased when she made the choice to pursue a PhD:

> When I went to do my PhD a lot of my aunts said to me, 'but when are you gonna get married? When are you gonna have children?' Even my mother, who I think she would have liked me to choose a more orthodox path in life, perhaps stop studying maybe at master's level, get married, have children, and I think that makes her nervous sometimes [...] So I think as a female my mum was a bit scared that, um, because men will say to me, 'no one is ever gonna marry you, no one wants somebody who is smart, who will challenge them', yeah [laughter]. It's like I've decreased my chances of being married by becoming educated.

Although the women whose stories are shared above were living lives that they deemed successful, other women in their families and communities struggled to accept that they had thus far prioritized their education and careers over marriage, even if they did desire marriage in the future. The participants reported that their fathers and other male relatives applied somewhat less pressure, though Neo was told by men in her community that she was making herself undesirable as a wife by pursuing a PhD. Speaking of women in China, Gaetano (2014: 126–7) writes, 'by seeming to prioritize education and career ahead of marriage and family, women who delay marriage challenge normative ideals of femininity and gender role, and thus their marital status garners more public scrutiny and social opprobrium'. Though the Chinese socioeconomic, cultural and historic context diverges from that of Botswana on many fronts, it is possible to trace global continuity in the social control of women through rigid gender norms related to marriage.

In cultural environments such as Botswana where the marital home is the cornerstone of the patriarchal order (Denbow and Thebe, 2006), women who have not married challenge the prevailing social order by demonstrating the possibility of surviving and even thriving autonomously. Such a challenge is liable to be met by resistance from women whose lives have been defined and constrained by the social order, perhaps in particular by those who have suffered as result, as in the cases of abuse and infidelity discussed above. Unmarried women are subjected to pressure and belittling comments about their single status from their female (usually married) seniors. In patriarchally ordered societies, women who remain single are viewed as inadequate or aberrant, an 'identity that requires justification' (Gaetano, 2014: 126). However, some of my participants felt unable to defend their single lifestyles, mindful that in doing so they risked being perceived as criticizing their elders' life choices. Community cohesion remains a powerful and necessary strength across Botswana and particularly in rural areas. While tolerating individual criticism serves social harmony, it comes at the cost of voicelessness.

Once a woman achieves the ultimate goal of marriage she is expected by her female seniors to stay married, with divorce affecting difficult social consequences. As already indicated, the pressure to remain in a marriage applies even in abusive unions (Maundeni, 2002). Lesedi had been encouraging her abused sister to leave her spouse for many years: 'Long I've told her, divorce this person and come back home', but her sister wanted to avoid divorce at all costs, which Lesedi attributed to the fear that 'if you can divorce you will be rejected somehow by the society'. Khana explained, 'here in Botswana, even if they are being abused in their marriage, to get out, for them, they don't believe in that'. Given that marriage brings a woman status, it becomes imperative for her to maintain her union to protect her social standing, especially among her married peers. Khana asserted, 'here in Botswana when you are married you are being respected. The problem is that, if that married man lets you down, and you run away, that's when [the women] say: "Ah, we were expecting that", but if you just cry and you hide your tears, they'll say: "This is a woman". Suffering silently is considered a badge of honour for a married woman, while 'even when you are not happy, if you divorce, you tend to be an outcast' (Malisa). Magistrate Kesegofetse reported that she sees numerous women coming through her court who are desperate to leave unhappy marriages, but 'cannot bring themselves to file for divorce' out of concern for the social consequences. Pono, who was married, spoke of the 'the shame of being a divorcee', equating divorce with profound moral failure.

In 1988 Kandiyoti coined the term 'patriarchal bargain' to describe a phenomenon in which women receive various forms of compensation in return for their submission to the patriarchal order, such as economic security and physical protection. In doing so, they 'avoid the normative order slipping away from them without any empowering alternatives' (Kandiyoti, 1988: 282–4). Since the normative order bestows women with social standing primarily through marriage and childbearing, older married mothers are compensated for a lifetime of compliance with respectability and authority over young and unmarried women. As such, shifting patterns in gender relations could be seen as threatening to their immediate interests. By putting pressure on unmarried women to get married and stay married, even in the presence of IPV, the senior female relatives of my participants are complicit in promoting and protecting a system that accommodates abuse. Wade (2011) summarized the patriarchal bargain as: 'a decision to accept gender rules that disadvantage women in exchange for whatever power one can wrest from the system. It is an individual strategy designed to manipulate the system to one's best advantage, but one that leaves the system itself intact.' Indeed, by prompting others to adhere to gendered cultural norms that disadvantage women, such as marriage at any cost, the senior female relatives of my participants are extracting empowerment for themselves within the gendered constraints of the system. Given the recognized importance of women as reproducers of culture, furthering our understanding of the ways women encourage compliance among other women in the Botswana context potentially illuminates avenues for social reform.

Motherhood makes a woman

While many of the participants considered marriage to be important for their standing in the community, achieving womanhood does not depend on just one mechanism. If marriage was unavailable, bearing children could bring adult status. In fact, much of the literature points to childbearing as the single most significant event in a woman's life. Schapera's early twentieth-century study (1938: 155) shows that 'marriage according to the Tswana is designed primarily for bearing children'. Such an emphasis on childbearing has continued to the present day, where 'womanhood is generally considered to be synonymous with motherhood'. In Datta's (2011: 130) research into fatherhood in urban Botswana, her focus-group participants 'overwhelmingly defined [women] in relation to motherhood'. In South Africa, too, Sennott and Mojola (2017: 7) found that 'biological motherhood was regarded as an important marker of womanhood', and Harrison and Montgomery (2001: 325) discovered that marriage and childbearing dominates women's narratives of their lives: 'In many cases, women's life histories *were* their reproductive histories'. Below I discuss the desire to bear children, the association of motherhood with womanhood, the transformational impact of childbearing on a woman's social and personal identity and the devastating effects of chronic infertility.

In the absence of a comprehensive welfare state children are viewed as a future source of both practical and economic support (Mogobe, 2005; Suggs, 1987; Upton and Myers Dolan, 2011), in addition to being 'objects of love' and 'continuation of family' (Suggs, 1987: 12). Despite the emotional and economic significance of children, total fertility in Botswana has seen a steady decline from 6.6 live births per woman in 1960 to 2.8 in 2021 (World Bank, 2022). The decline has been attributed to several intersecting forces, such as women's increasing education and access to formal employment, urbanization patterns and lower infant mortality rates (World Bank, 2010: viii). Botswana's fertility decline can be situated in the context of global fertility decline: live births per woman more than halved between 1960 and 2016, from a global average of 5 to 2.4, and have remained static since (World Bank, 2022). Among my participants, 23 per cent of the participants had no children at all, 37 per cent had one child, 27 per cent had two children, 10 per cent had three children, none had four children and only 3 per cent had five children. None had more than five children. Total fertility rates are globally higher for rural women than urban women, and there is a negative correlation between education level and fertility (World Bank, 2010: 5). This pattern is reflected among the women in my study: five of the seven participants who had no children were highly educated urban women. The only participant with five children (Laone) was rural and had secondary education. Despite relatively low fertility rates, the desire for children was almost uniform across my sample; just one participant who did not have children did not wish to become a mother (Keeya). National fertility decline notwithstanding, the desire to bear children was close to uniform for the women I interviewed who did not have children.

Mogobe (2005: 33) asserts that a girl 'consciously and unconsciously internalizes what it means to be a woman in Botswana' in response to what she is told and what she sees – that bearing children will make her a woman. Such a view was common among my sample: eighteen of my participants thought that womanhood status would be achieved upon becoming a mother, for that is when 'it is thought that now you are a *real* woman' (Pono). Taemane was unequivocal about what she saw as the immutable association of motherhood with womanhood: 'A woman is supposed to have children. That is what it means. Motherhood [...] if you look at a woman you see a mother. That is what it means.' Along with marriage, bearing a child was considered a prerequisite for being perceived as a woman in the community. With womanhood status comes respectability; others would relate differently to those who had a child. Ona celebrated motherhood 'because people respect somebody who has children, it makes you a woman, it makes people take you a certain way', and Akhu reported that as 'a mother you tend to get a little bit more respect'. Emelda described similar views: 'Motherhood is a good thing. To other people [...] If they see and they know that you are a mother, they respect that.' Pono explained why she thought motherhood was necessary for being seen as a woman: 'When you have a child, you start to love in a different way, you know, that unconditional love. The focus is not always on you, now it goes to the children [...] and that makes you a woman.' Her view illustrates the value of the gendered social construct of self-sacrificing mother, common in many parts of the world. In the Global North, too, self-sacrifice is embodied in the construction of motherhood, which 'emerges as a significant moral enterprise'

(Park, 2002: 25). I further examine the self-sacrificing feminine ideal in the next chapter.

The respect afforded to biological mothers is illustrated linguistically, with women receiving a new term of address upon bearing their first child. Formerly called by their first name, new mothers are given the title of *Mma* ('mother') followed by the name of their child. This practice is a mark of respect and is widely adopted: participants from rural and urban areas and of different ages and backgrounds had either experienced the change themselves or had witnessed it in their communities. The new name is used by the community at large but also by close friends and relatives to denote status. Considering the meaning of being called by her child's name, Thato reflected: 'They realise that I have grown up. I have grown up, I am *Mma* Kaelo, when I get home my child is home.' Here the home plays a central role in the construction of female adulthood. Though women in Botswana have historically worked outside of the home as agricultural labourers and are today often engaged in formal or informal employment, the home is still considered their 'rightful' place, the site where they raise their children and care for their husbands. In fact, 'woman' translates to *mosadi* in Setswana, meaning 'the one who stays' (Suggs, 1987). Given the high rates of population movement and distributed households, 'the one who stays' might appear a somewhat incongruous conceptualization. However, it serves as illustrative of the resilience of gendered ideology in the face of conflicting external realities.

Naledi shared how her new name indicated a respectable new relational identity, one that she was proud of: 'I think when we have a child they respect you more than when you don't have [a child]. They will think, "This one now is *Mma* of, the mother of ... " We mean the mother of, or somebody's mother.' Similarly, Sefela spoke of her pride when 'people see you out there and they know that you are the mother of whoever'. While waiting to conceive for the first time, Lesedi had 'wanted to be called "auntie" at least, because' she 'didn't have a kid by then'. For her, this meant, 'even if you don't know me, you'll never know I don't have a kid because I will be "auntie"'. Although Lesedi was not yet eligible for the title of *Mma*, she was able to substitute it with an alternative term that still implied a role in child caregiving and had the effect of concealing her childlessness in public spaces.[4] While not as desirable as *Mma*, Lesedi still considered the title 'auntie' preferable to being called by her forename because of its close connotations with motherhood. Auntie is a term of respect in Botswana that does not necessarily have any relation to biological aunthood. Upon bearing her first child, Lesedi was delighted to be renamed in reference to her motherhood status because of the impact it had on people's attitudes towards her. She recalled: 'After I gave birth they know I'm called "*Mma* Tshwanelo". I was happy of that.' Though Lesedi embraced her new name, she did struggle to get used to it initially. She recalled with laughter: 'The very first time when I got home from the hospital my father just said, "*Mma* Tshwanelo", since then he called me *Mma* Tshwanelo until the day he died. And you know, what's funny about it was, I even forget that I'm *Mma* Tshwanelo! You know, when you call, "*Mma* Tshwanelo!", huh, who?'

Like Lesedi, Tumelo also found it difficult to connect her new name with her own sense of self and did not recognize it initially. However, unlike Lesedi, she spoke about the change in a despondent tone:

> They will call you by your child's name, and then they address you as if, with a little bit of respect. Sometimes when they say, 'Ah, *Mma* Karabo, this and this and that' I will just ignore the person until they repeat themselves, '*Mma* Karabo, I said this and this and that' and I'll be, 'oh, she is talking to me'.

When I asked Tumelo how it felt to have others bestow a new name upon her, she shrugged and said she had not considered her feelings on the matter because 'it's just what you do'. Thato found the change challenging. She disliked it at first and found it frustrating but became accustomed to it eventually: 'At first hey, I never used to like it, because they used to call me by *my* name. I don't know, I think it's fine now. It's fine.' Tsala was unusual among my interviewees in her vocal resentment of the custom: 'I have lost my name, you know? I'm Tsala! You know? I have lost that. Now I am identified as *Mma* Anele, and though it's cultural, and a way of showing respect, I kind of differ, I say that I'm Anele's mother, but I'm Tsala, I'm myself. Identify me as who I am, not whose mother am I.' Tsala developed a strategy that allowed her to protect her sense of self without explicitly challenging custom; she introduced herself as Tsala to new people and used Tsala as her written name, while responding to 'Mma Anele' when addressed in such a way. This compromise gave her a sense of agency while preserving social harmony.

Upon becoming pregnant Tshiamo was immediately, definitively and visibly re-categorized as an adult by her church, a significant organizing institution in rural areas: 'In our church when you have a child you are not allowed to take sacrament. And I was cut from taking the sacrament, and I was excluded from the choir of the, the youth choir. I was supposed to carry out adult activities only. Going to Thursday churches of the ladies, you know.' Though Tshiamo had her first child as an adolescent following an unplanned pregnancy, she was no longer considered a youth in the eyes of her community. Tshiamo found this shift challenging; having struggled with the upheaval of an unplanned pregnancy, she was then separated from her peers and prevented from taking part in an activity she enjoyed. When I asked her how her life had changed upon having children, this social repositioning was the only thing she spoke of, implying that it had a profound effect on her, and was perhaps her most enduring memory of the experience of becoming a mother for the first time. Tshiamo's story illustrates the effect that bearing children has on others' perceptions of women, and the ways in which active measures are taken to situate women in spaces deemed appropriate to their status.

While all my participants said that women gain new social standing upon becoming a mother, Mabedi (aged twenty-six) and Malisa (aged forty-three) were quick to qualify that their own mothers did not change their attitude towards them once they had given birth. Though both were rewarded with newfound respect in their communities, they were treated as minors within their mother's households, where each lived with their children. Mabedi and Malisa were both unmarried with one child and lived in rural areas. Mabedi complained that her mother still treated her as 'a girl [...] still sent to do whatever it is that needs to be done in the house'. Malisa lamented that 'if you are a child, even if you are 50 years [old], if you are a child to somebody you are still a child', motioning towards her mother who was seated nearby. However, she asserted that upon bearing a child, others in the village 'will just tend to respect you as an elderly person, not like the small girl you used to be'. It appears that the line between girl and woman can be fluid and situational, a boundary that shifts in the filial context. Whether establishing an independent household was deemed necessary for women to view their childbearing offspring as adults would be a worthy area of further investigation, particularly given the widespread economic constraints on doing so.

Pamela construed the association of motherhood with womanhood in terms of sexual maturity, or rather, with the public assumption of sexual maturity. Becoming pregnant made a woman's sexual activity evident: 'Um, in Botswana when you have a child that's when they say you are a woman. Before then you can be treated as a child. As soon as you get pregnant they'll be like, "Oh, she grown now! She be having sex!", yeah ... so that's when they say, "Oh, she's a woman now, she's having sex".' The potential for ambiguity around the connection between sexual activity and pregnancy, such as in cases of rape, was not acknowledged; when Pamela became pregnant at a very young age it was assumed that she had been engaging in consensual sex. Pamela's view is difficult to frame in the context of my interviews because none of the other participants mentioned sex as an indicator of having achieved womanhood. However, it is likely that sex is considered a function of adulthood because it facilitates childbearing.

Christoforou's (2018: 50) study of menstruation among Greek Cypriot women demonstrated that the first occurrence of menstruation is 'a rite of passage, a sign of "becoming a woman", and "being completed as a woman"', in part because it signifies fertility. Likewise, six of my participants said that a girl becomes a woman once she starts puberty: 'Now you have your periods you are a woman, because you can mother a kid' (Lesedi). Although the other five participants did not make this connection explicit, the context of what they said gave me the impression that puberty is regarded as a significant life stage because it indicates potential fertility. For these participants, like the other women in my study, marriage and motherhood were the primary markers of full womanhood status. Yet, the perceived biological ability to become pregnant represented a significant shift in the direction of adulthood. This view was not contingent on particular demographic variables – rural and urban participants aged twenty-five to forty-three spoke of menstruation as a conspicuous signifier that full womanhood was approaching. Suggs (1987) also found that a girl was considered to become a woman upon her first menstruation but would not be bestowed full adulthood status until she had given birth and could manage her own household. Upon their first period, girls were told they must act differently – keep clean, play less and focus on their responsibilities in the home in preparation for adulthood.

While bearing children is considered a marker of womanhood, taking care of the children of others can also increase one's social standing. Laone said 'being a woman is [only] when you have a child', but that a particularly noteworthy woman would be one who 'mother[s] every child out there'. Likewise, Naledi described women as 'the ones who raise our children', and Pono defined a woman's role as 'help[ing] to raise, you know, our young people, the children'. The expectation that women will care for all children in the community supports the finding that Batswana rely on extended kin networks for childrearing (Smith, 2013), a norm common in Black communities globally (Uttal, 1999). While women are unlikely to achieve adulthood status through the caretaking of others' children alone, such behaviour could enhance their standing in the community, providing an alternative route to respectability for those who were childless or childfree. However, the gendered expectation that all women will participate in communal 'mothering' creates an involuntary burden of labour and other resources.

The implications of childlessness

As a childfree woman in her twenties at the time of my research for this book and for my previous research in the country, I was frequently interrogated by women demanding to know when I would be having children. My insistence that I had no desire to become pregnant now or in the future was met with incredulity. One interviewee from my earlier study exclaimed, 'it's weird. It's strange. How can a human being, a woman, not want children?' (Smith, 2013: 171). The notion that any woman would remain childfree voluntarily was inconceivable to some, particular in reference to Batswana women: 'when you're a Motswana woman [...] you will have children [...] if you dare mention that you're not interested in having children, whoa! What?!' (Smith, 2013: 171). Being voluntarily childfree is unusual in Botswana, particularly insofar as it remains a lifelong choice. Emelda struggled to relate to women who did not want children, and stressed that 'it's rare, it's very rare [...] for a woman to say, "I don't want a child"'. She believed that choosing not to have children was only for 'those ones who are lesbians'; the notion of choosing not to bear children was incompatible with her heteronormative notion of womanhood and she considered it 'unnatural', aligning with De Beauvoir's (1949: 537) notion that 'it is through motherhood that woman fully achieved her physiological destiny; that is her "natural" vocation'. Reneilwe shared Emelda's view, and that of many of my interviewees, when she asserted that 'women should start having babies' because it is 'the natural thing' for them to do.

Except for Keeya, all of my participants either had children or said that they wanted to become mothers eventually. Keeya, however, explained that she had 'never really had that sort of maternal thing where you want to like, have kids'. She reported that she was comfortable with her choice, but that others were not: 'A lot of people ask me [...] those things don't weigh down on me at all, but other people are like, "Oh no".' While she did not feel personally affected by the external pressure she was subjected to, she recognized the difficulties such a burden might cause for other women: 'It would be nice if women could, you know, have more of a say in regards to just not wanting kids at all, because you know, Botswana is still the place where if you're a woman you should have children.' Thus, to remain childfree is to threaten the fundamental ideology upon which gendered social relations have been constructed – that women are biological reproducers. As Keeya's story illustrates, such a challenge can create tension between a woman and her community. The social difficulties faced by women who do not want to be mothers are not unique to Botswana – choosing not to have children is problematic in pronatalist cultures worldwide (Park, 2002).

All but one of my childless or childfree participants felt pressured to become mothers and fulfil their culturally prescribed function as biological reproducers. Neo, a thirty-year-old urban postgraduate with no children, explained that although many women were encouraged to get an education and pursue a career, it was on the understanding that motherhood would be prioritized: 'People are like, "When are you gonna have a child?" [...] because the priority is your biological clock, and you need to have a child.' The statistics support the notion that education is endorsed for women and girls; more women receive university education than men, for example, with a gender parity index of 1.36 for tertiary school enrolment (World Bank, 2022). Yet, pursuing education and a vocational career was socially acceptable only insofar as it did not interfere with motherhood. In my earlier study of attitudes to abortion in contemporary urban Botswana, I found that while many of the women I interviewed wanted to pursue their careers or education and were supported in that by their families, such pursuits were limited to the space around childbearing. For instance, it was considered unacceptable to delay childbearing or to end a pregnancy because of career commitments (Smith, 2013). Keeya put it plainly: 'if you're a woman, you have kids.'

Basadi felt 'no real pressure from anyone' to become a mother, but she was unique among the participants in this respect. Basadi was raised in Botswana's capital, Gaborone, and had gained her higher education in the United States and the United Kingdom before moving back to Botswana where she worked in the creative industry. Other women in my study who were urban, well-travelled, highly educated and were enjoying vocational careers reported feeling unyielding social pressure to bear children, suggesting that those might not be differentiating factors in Basadi's case. At twenty-seven, Basadi was among the youngest of my participants. Perhaps she had not yet reached the age where becoming *mafetwa* was a concern for those in her community. Pressure to bear children began by the mid-twenties for the rural women in my sample whereas the margin for urban women was slightly wider, allowing for the possibility of completing further education and establishing a career before embarking on motherhood. Though the women in my study who were pursuing higher education or vocational careers still felt social pressure to become mothers eventually, space was held for additional identities in a way that it was not for resource-poor women, who did not have access to further education or formal employment. Similarly in Bangladesh 'motherhood appears to be the main or only culturally available social identity for women' (Nahar and Richters, 2011: 328), but the social pressure to bear children is felt most keenly among rural women, where limited education and employment options mean that 'only motherhood can provide a woman with a respectable identity' (Nahar and Richters, 2011: 334).

Lesedi's story illustrates the very real consequences of the social coercion to have a child that she experienced as relentless: 'I had my first-born when I was 30, and honestly speaking I'll say it was the pressure of the society, the societal pressure, you see. Being this age without having a kid, I had no choice but to [have a child].' Once she gave birth it was considered that she had fulfilled one of the two primary requirements of her prescribed role as a woman in the community and she could 'relax' somewhat; while the people in her life would lament that she was unmarried, they would concede, 'at least you have a kid'. Shera had spent time studying in Northern Europe prior to our interview. Reflecting upon the pressures she was experiencing upon her return to Botswana, she exclaimed, 'even the last two weeks, the number of people who have asked me, "When are you having children?" [...] In the last two weeks more people have asked than in the last year in Europe'. Though expectations on women to bear children are pervasive around the globe, Shera's story illuminates how local culture shapes the prioritization of gendered norms to the extent that 'motherhood is rather a mandate and not an option' (Mogobe, 2005: 33). Shera concluded, 'I don't think women feel like they can self-determine' having children. Kesegofetse elaborated on the social consequences of failing to 'follow the defined channel' of getting married and becoming a mother: 'society starts judging you and sees you as a lesser woman than what you are.' Thus, marriage and or motherhood are prerequisites for being valued as a 'full' woman or 'complete' woman, and women without children are viewed as inferior or deviant. Likewise, 90 per cent of the women Suggs (1987) interviewed in Mochudi, one of the villages where I conducted interviews, claimed that a woman without children was not complete.

For Batswana women who cannot have children because of real or perceived infertility, the social consequences are devastating (Mogobe, 2005; Schapera, 1938; Upton, 2001; Upton and Myers Dolan, 2011). Studies in Zimbabwe, Nigeria, Bangladesh, Australia, the United States and elsewhere lend evidence to the argument that women are stigmatized globally for being unable to conceive, suffering exclusion, shame and humiliation in their communities (Folkvord et al., 2005; Hollos et al., 2009; Jansen and Onge, 2015; Nahar and Richters, 2011; Turnbull et al., 2016). In Bangladesh the stigma of childlessness is epitomized by the common proverb, 'even a fox or a dog does not eat the dead body of a childless woman' (Nahar and Richters, 2011: 331). In Botswana an infertile person is given the derogatory term *moopa, meopa* or *moopana*, and is described as 'desiccated or dried up, as useless, sterile and even as having transgressed some boundaries of normal Tswana behaviour, as mentally and physically ill and disabled' (Upton and Myers Dolan, 2011: 97). Upton and Myers Dolan's findings reflect Schapera's (1938) historic interpretation of the social effects of perceived infertility: 'If a woman fails in this important duty her lot is hard. She receives little sympathy as a rule; her husband neglects or ill-treats her; she is scorned by other men and ridiculed by her own sex.' Women who cannot bear children are socially penalized and seen as incomplete. An infertile woman is derided and disrespected by both men and women in her community; if it is thought that she is incapable of bearing children, she faces lasting humiliation (Gage-Brandon and Meekers, 1993; Phaladze and Tlou, 2006; Schapera, 1938). Upton and Myers Dolan (2011) found that women's concerns about possible infertility did not necessarily stem from not being able to bear children, but from fear of the accompanying stigma. My interviews supported these findings; the women I interviewed who could not conceive spoke of being publicly humiliated, blamed, gossiped about and accused of deviant behaviours. None of them talked about receiving support or empathy.

Taemane had always wanted to have children and at forty-three did not understand why she had never become pregnant. In addition to her personal grief over being unable to conceive, she was subjected to local gossip and intrusive questions about her fertility: 'They talk about it, they ask "why she doesn't have children?" [...] assuming I can't conceive or something.' Keatlaretse explained that before she had had her son, her community thought she 'couldn't have kids [...] a big taboo'. She was ridiculed: 'You turn out to be a laughingstock [...] yeah so it was, it's not a good space.' Keatlaretse was rejected and embarrassed, her femininity and identity as a woman undermined: 'They believe that you are not a woman if you don't have a child, you know.' Upton (2001: 349, 354) maintains that in Botswana, 'individuals who are perceived as infertile run the risk of becoming culturally invisible and challenge the very concept of personhood and social identity', for, 'in a country where childbearing has long been a central aspect of gender identity, the perception that one is infertile can be devastating for social status'. Similarly in Nigeria, while 'nominal womanhood' may be realized through age or marriage, childbearing brings full adult status and 'represents normative fulfilment of what is considered to be female destiny' (Hollos et al., 2009: 2068). In Butler's (1988: 520) conceptualization of gender performance as an 'accomplishment compelled by social sanction and taboo', 'those who fail to do their gender right are regularly punished' (522). Framed in this way, it follows that women who cannot have children are socially penalized in a culture where womanhood is largely defined by a person's ability to give birth.

Historically infertility was ascribed to: 'Sorcery, to some deficiency in the woman's "blood", to some abnormality of her womb, to some former abortion, and, above all, to the fact that before marriage she had led a very promiscuous life' (Schapera, 1938: 155). Klaits (1997: 328) found that in general, 'bodily suffering is seen as an aspect of diseased social relations'. These beliefs remain alongside more contemporary attributions, such as the use of modern contraception, drug and alcohol use, breaking sexual taboos, having sex before marriage and God's will (Upton and Myers Dolan, 2011). If social and sexual taboos are understood to be the cause of infertility, it follows that a woman who cannot conceive 'risk[s] characterisation as an individual who is not seen as a Motswana, who is invisible in social life' (Upton, 2001: 354). Emelda spoke of a forty-year-old friend of hers who had not been able to conceive, and who was 'bereft without a kid'. She elaborated: 'When you are 40 without a child, right now, people are trying to, they treat you in a bad way. They say, "Oh, maybe she was doing many abortions, that's why she doesn't have a child." They won't even look at other reasons why you don't have a child. It's just [seen as] unnatural.' Abortions are restricted by law in Botswana and are highly taboo, with women who terminate their pregnancies condemned as murderous and Godless (Mogwe, 1992; Smith, 2013). As such, Emelda's friend was subjected to both the grief of childlessness and the pain of social ostracization.

Cultural norms around infertility dictate that men cannot be sterile; a couple's inability to conceive must therefore be attributed to a moral or physical problem on the woman's part (Upton and Myers Dolan, 2011). Keatlaretse explained, 'this thing of checking at the clinic if it's because of the man, you know, they don't believe in that. Yeah so most of the time they just rush into pointing the finger at the woman.' Keatlaretse said it would be difficult for a woman to suggest that her male partner might be infertile: 'Most of the time you can't say that […] it's more like you are being disrespectful […] it doesn't sit well. Somehow it can be taken as, that they are not men.' This suggests that just as female infertility undermines a woman's femininity, male infertility presents a challenge to masculinity. Yet, the consequences of such a view are gendered; women are expected to take responsibility for problems conceiving while men escape blame, regardless of which partner might be sterile. Given that childless women suffer condemnation and exclusion, they are placed in a particularly unjust position if their male partner is infertile and are denied their gendered identity (Mogobe, 2005). Reneilwe concluded that because women are 'defined by being able to bear kids [...] they will always blame women'.

Mogobe (2005) contends that seemingly infertile women suffer reprimand and abuse from in-laws and are encouraged to allow their husbands access to another woman, perhaps a family member, so that children can be brought into the home. While this brings emotional distress, some women might consider it preferable to desertion by her husband or partner. However, such an approach will inevitably fail if the fertility issues sit with the husband or partner. When this is thought to be the case, such as when a woman has been able to conceive with a previous partner but not with the man she is with now, or if the man has never conceived a child despite having unprotected sex with multiple partners, it is known that she might employ creative strategies to bring about a culturally acceptable solution. A participant in Upton's (2011) study had birthed two children in the past but had not conceived in the last several years. Her community assumed she had committed some transgression, such as witchcraft, and had become infertile. Her husband worked in the mines and was absent for long periods. Eventually she conceived a third child when her husband was absent, which she claimed to have carried for the fourteen months since her husband was last home. She explained to Upton that the baby was a 'sleeping foetus' who was not ready to leave the womb, and insisted that it was her husband's child. Her culturally appropriate narrative was accepted and she was able to escape undue blame for her perceived infertility, becoming 'visible' again as a woman in her community.

While extramarital childbearing once brought social penalties for both parties, the reality of declining marriage rates meant that by the 1980s it had become largely permissible, if undesirable (Izzard, 1985; Suggs, 1987). Lesedi described people's reluctant acceptance of her single motherhood:

> Some people will have an eye on you, you see, 'she has kids without being married', but anyway, it's just the normal thing [...] somebody of my age is

expected to be married and having all the kids at their own house, but I don't have that, but it is normal, it is common among most of us Batswana to be [single mothers].

Though Lesedi experienced occasional judgement within her community for being an unmarried mother, it was far less severe than the condemnation she had suffered as a woman without children. Neo explained that 'the acceptance of single mothers is much better now [because] once you get past thirty there's an unspoken rule where it would be okay just to have a child out of wedlock'. While cultural ideals favour childbearing within marriage, extramarital childbearing is preferable to having no children at all. Likewise, among women in rural Mpumalanga Province, South Africa, it is considered 'more important to have children, even if it happens at a less than ideal time, than to not have children at all' (Sennott and Mojola, 2017: 7). I discuss single motherhood in more detail in the next chapter.

While the perception of marriage as the most appropriate site for childbearing remains, the reality is that 'marriage and childbearing have become increasingly separate domains of life' (Suggs, 1987: 354). However, while 'one need not be married to have a child [...] one may need to have a child in order to get married' (Suggs, 1987: 354). A man and his kin prefer his wife to have had at least one child prior to marriage, either by him or another man, thereby demonstrating her fertility before they commit to taking her into the family (Suggs, 1987; Upton, 2001). Reneilwe, who had no children, explained that a man's family would pressure him to end a relationship with a childless woman like her: 'They will say, "Ah my son, can't you look for someone who can [have children], I want grandchildren".' Keatlaretse had problems forming relationships with men before she had her first child: 'They don't get attracted to you. Come to him and say I don't have a child, they think you can't [conceive]. So they run away.' The preference for brides who have proven their fertility is common in sub-Saharan Africa (Mokomane, 2005). Upton and Myers Dolan (2011: 91) found that 'in every recorded narrative, Tswana (both fertile and infertile) *always* stated that having children in order to get married, stay married and to be seen as a successful person in Botswana was necessary above all else'.

Marriage and childbearing: An overview

Achieving recognition as a woman in the community is dependent on marriage and childbearing, available only through the relational identities of wife and mother. Thus, social status and visibility for women are closely tied to their relationships with men and to cultural values informed by patriarchy. The requirements for achieving 'womanhood' limit women's ability to self-define independent identities, for to do so they must evade or reject social norms; the consequences of remaining unmarried or without children range from familial pressure to outright ostracization. The expectation that women will shape their lives around marriage and motherhood is at odds with the realities of declining marriage and fertility rates. Wifehood and motherhood are less desirable and less attainable than they once were, and alternative identities are newly available to women with resources. Yet, the necessity of both in being deemed as a respectable adult in the community is pervasive, affecting women of all ages and backgrounds in both rural and urban areas. Womanhood is associated with a significant burden of labour in the realms of domestic work and formal employment, kin and community, character and appearance, and managing male dominance. I explore the costs of womanhood in the next chapter.

Notes

1   When speaking about 'becoming a woman' or 'achieving womanhood', my participants were typically describing the transition from female youth to female adult. Thus, I have followed their lead here in using 'womanhood' and 'adulthood' interchangeably in the context of such a transition, while acknowledging that both terms are historically and culturally specific and are not interchangeable in all settings.

2   Note, the figures cited by Sardinha et al. (2022) exclude emotional and psychological violence and controlling behaviour, which are more difficult to quantify and measure.

3   However, it is not possible to ascertain from the study results whether this was an effect of higher likelihood of reporting among women who are educated and employed.

4   I use the term 'childless' in this book to describe women who want to have children but are prevented from doing so by circumstances beyond their control, for example, infertility. I use 'childfree' to denote those for whom not having children is a deliberate and voluntary decision. In cases where it was unclear if a particular participant was childless or childfree, I use 'without children' and similar phrases.

4

'I keep on feeling like they take advantage': The costs of womanhood

–Keatlaretse

Whether or not womanhood is fully realized and socially acknowledged through marriage and motherhood, the weight of expectation on women is considerable. Outside of the gender-defining obligations of marriage and childbearing, women are required to demonstrate their respectability carrying out a litany of domestic tasks, participating in formal and informal waged labour, getting an education, raising their own and others' children, fulfilling their partner or husband's sexual and other needs on demand, managing cultural codes of dress and appearance and providing an extensive range of services for their relatives and the wider community. The successful performance of respectable womanhood depends on meeting these requirements within the constraints of male dominance and in a manner that demonstrates hegemonic femininity, described by Schippers (2007: 94) as consisting of 'characteristics defined as womanly that establish and legitimate a hierarchical and complementary relationship to hegemonic masculinity and that, by doing so, guarantee the dominant position of men and the subordination of women'. The cost of compliance is materially and emotionally high, as Keatlaretse epitomized: 'I keep on feeling like they take advantage. And I'm at a stage where I really, really wish I was somewhere else.'

The burden of domestic labour

Throughout history gender arrangements have attributed the domestic realm to women, with conventional notions about the division of labour serving to define women as housewives and caregivers (Connell and Pearse, 2015). Though the second part of the twentieth century saw women moving into the global market economy, they nonetheless continue to be held responsible for most domestic work and childcare around the world (Connell and Pearse, 2015). In the United States, for example, 'the gender division of household labor remains strikingly unequal', with women spending twice as much time on housework and childcare as their male partners (Ridgeway, 2011: 128). Household labour was a major feature of daily life for the participants in my study, regardless of their socioeconomic position, marital status, whether they were mothers and whether they were formally or informally employed outside of the home. All the women I interviewed were responsible for a myriad of tasks that they experienced as overwhelming. The specific tasks required varied between those living in urban areas with modern amenities and those living in villages without running water or electricity and were thus class-informed as well as gender-informed. Women from both urban and rural areas reported the duties of 'cleaning, washing, cooking' (Ona); 'sweeping outside and inside' (Elizabeth); 'ironing' (Tumelo); 'laundry' (Mabedi); feeding and 'bathing the kids' (Thato); preparing children for school, helping with 'the homework' and putting them to bed (Tsala) and 'make sure the bills are paid, make sure there is food in the house … ' (Tumelo). For rural women who had access to fewer facilities, additional tasks included 'making a fire with firewood' for warmth, cooking and heating water (Sefela), and 'get[ting] the water' for drinking, cooking, cleaning and washing clothes (Laone). Women living in traditional round huts were also responsible for resurfacing floors and fortifying walls and roofs as required. For many of the participants, domestic labour was required 'every day, all day' (Sefela).

Tumelo elaborated on her daily priorities: 'The duties are things like to sweep, to clean, to cook, to bath babies, take them to school, find school for them, pay the school fees, make sure the bills are paid, make sure there is food in the house. The man will just be giving you money, you go buy the food […] man the house, that's all.' That Tumelo used the expression 'man the house' to denote housework and childcare was important; in the context of a patriarchal society the phrase suggested a leadership role for women in the home sphere. Yet, the compulsory nature of her domestic obligations undermined her agency in the role; she managed the household and spent the money her partner earned as required for the family, however, the finances ultimately remained in his control, with him meting out funds when he agreed they were needed. Thus, while women might achieve a level of influence within the household, their basic economic dependence remains a constraint to their autonomy.

Several women described their domestic burdens as a defining feature of the 'wifely' role. Given that most of my interviewees were unmarried, the association of their household labour with wifeliness suggests the presence of a culturally constructed feminine identity – 'the good wife' – that exists independently of marital status. If a good wife makes an ideal woman, then it follows that wifely duties are necessary for the ongoing performance of womanhood inside or outside of marriage. Further, the connotation of competent household management and childcare with wifeliness perhaps indicates that the anticipation of finding a husband was at the forefront of daily activities. That is not to suggest that women consciously accept an unequal burden of domestic labour because they believe that it will lead to marriage; very few of my interviewees indicated that rejecting or negotiating such a burden was a possibility for action. Rather, the execution of wifely duties was a gender-conforming practice that signified readiness for marriage in the cultural sphere. A Black South African friend of mine described her intensive household labour as an ongoing 'audition' for her boyfriend, believing he would recognize her excellence in household management as proof of her aptitude as a wife. Indeed, Schapera (1938) observed that women were encouraged to practise their marital duties in advance of any union through the domestic service of their male relatives and older female relatives.

Being a 'good wife' means, among other things, ensuring that a husband always finds his home clean and his meals prepared on his preferred schedule. Mpho commented on the advice given to this end by married women in the customary pre-marital meetings designed for instructing new brides:

> Mpho: You're basically told how to be a good wife. Yeah. And what to do to make him happy.
>
> Researcher: What kinds of things are you supposed to do to make him happy?
>
> Mpho: Well, you know, cooking and cleaning. As soon as he comes in the door you should have his food ready.

Mpho, a young independent urban woman with an undergraduate degree and a demanding full-time administration job, anticipated receiving similar counsel herself once she became engaged. Her elders expected her to take on a servile role upon marriage regardless of her pre-marital autonomy, demonstrating the power of the institution to transform gender arrangements within the domestic sphere. Reneilwe, a young rural woman with formal employment in the capital, spoke of similar advice she had been given: 'You get married, they tell you, "Men should be prepared food".' Recognition of these norms was ubiquitous among the women I spoke to, who were all either fulfilling a servile role in the home already or anticipated being expected to do so once partnered, regardless of where they were from or whether they lived independently. The participants' accounts reflect Schapera's (1940: 95) observation that a woman on the cusp of marriage was told to 'pay formal deference' to her new husband as his *motlhanka* (servant), 'speaking to him respectfully, waiting on him, serving him first with food', indicating continuity of gender regimes in the household over the past century.

Though the acknowledgement that a woman is supposed to be servile and deferential towards her husband, other men and older women in the household was universal among my participants, attitudes towards this arrangement varied – some women embraced or defended it while others challenged or resented it; the majority appeared resigned to its inevitability. Taemane, who was forty-three and single, delighted at the notion of serving a husband. Framing the role in an explicitly gendered way, she declared that she 'would give her love, respect him, and do everything that needs to be done as the woman for her husband. Clothe him, feed him, cook for him'. Taemane said that she was desperate to be married and had idealized the position of the subservient wife since she was a small child. Taemane had received only primary education and had lived alone with her mother in rural Morwa all her life. Though she had been able to secure one of very few formal employment positions available in her village, it was part-time and paid barely enough for her to buy food for herself and her mother. Taemane's lack of education severely limited her options for formal employment, and with her existing funds tightly stretched, she could not afford to travel to find work in other parts of the country. In Taemane's idealized version of marriage, the husband was a successful breadwinner. Perhaps the possibility of financial security contributed to Taemane's self-described all-consuming desire to take the role of subordinate wife; her dedicated labour might ultimately secure her survival in ways that formal employment had not.

Reneilwe was almost twenty years younger than Taemane but their attitudes towards the gendered division of household labour were well aligned. In fact, Reneilwe vehemently defended the cultural norm. When I asked her if she would prefer a future husband to contribute to the household labour she seemed confused, as if she found the concept inconceivable. After a moment's reflection she exclaimed,

> What is it going to look like? […] it's going to kill the family! That man won't have trust in the woman. Won't have faith in the family. He's always complaining: 'Ah, this woman, she doesn't know what is right for women, she doesn't know how to take care of me as her husband' […] Obviously, if it's a man with a heart, if it's a woman with a heart, it won't be fine.

For Reneilwe, the division of labour along gendered lines went right to the core of what it meant to be a family. Reneilwe's conservative view was particularly noteworthy considering she held an information and communications technology (ICT) internship in the capital city. Women are a minority in the science, technology, engineering, and mathematics (STEM) sector worldwide and are 'grossly underrepresented' in STEM fields in sub-Saharan Africa, including in Botswana (Marie-Nelly, 2021). Reneilwe was seeking to establish herself in a field where women's presence is challenged by gender biases and discriminatory practices, yet she unequivocally supported unequal gender norms in the domestic realm. At twenty-five she was my youngest interviewee. As I discuss in the next chapter, new generations typically lead in reshaping traditional practices that no longer serve them, and this was apparent in Reneilwe's choice of career in a male-dominated field. However, she had no desire to modify or challenge cultural expectations of women in the household space.

In their absolute support of an inequitable burden of labour for women in the household, Reneilwe and Taemane were in the minority among the women I interviewed. Most of my participants resented the expectation that women would do the lion's share of domestic work within marriage and in advance of it, regardless of their background variables. Solway (2016: 314–15) similarly found that many women 'now chafe at the idea of joining their husband's family as subordinates' once they marry. Thato lamented that as a woman 'you have to do everything [...] the husband just sits there and expects you to do everything [...] it should change, it should be 50/50 because we are all human beings'. Like Thato, most of the participants who discussed household labour reported that men do not and or should not participate in domestic work or childcare. When I asked Thato if she would prefer her husband to do more in their home she explained that while she would appreciate his assistance, 'according to my culture I wouldn't allow that. Like yeah, he can help washing dishes when I'm not feeling well, or bath the child when I'm not feeling well, but when I'm okay I do things myself.' Her husband sharing in the housework or childcare was a last resort, only appropriate when Thato was physically unable to do it herself. Tumelo expressed her frustration with her fiancé, who refused to do housework on the grounds that it was women's work: 'What I want is I want to see a situation whereby my husband will understand that I'm also a human being [...] If I clean the house, he should at least do the laundry. If I iron, he should at least cook.' Her husband disagreed, asserting that the gendered division of household labour was 'how things are supposed to be done'. Though Tumelo was comfortable challenging her fiancé to do more domestic labour, she felt that ultimately she had no choice but to accept his stance. Thato and Tumelo were both university-educated women in their early thirties, with one child each and permanent jobs in professional industries. Though they were financially independent and vocationally successful, they felt personally diminished by the inequitable labour division at home. Importantly, in the context of household work both Thato and Tumelo felt the need to stress that women are human beings; they experienced the gendered expectation of subservience as a challenge to their innate humanity.

While the cultural construction of womanhood defines women's position as homemakers, it also explicitly excludes men from the role. Datta's (2011) focus group and interview-based research into fatherhood in urban Botswana illuminated men's perspectives on labour in the home. Her male participants largely rejected housework, preferring to 'just go out and get drunk' instead (Datta, 2011: 131). Those who would consider assisting women with domestic tasks were prevented from doing so by family members attempting to guard the status quo (Datta, 2011). Comparably, my interviews indicated that a man who helped with the chores would be subject to gossip within the community. Lesedi elaborated: 'A woman is expected to go to the kitchen to do the household chores [...] And there is this belief that if a man is seen doing the household chores it's like, they could even say, they will say it in Setswana, "you are not man enough, why are you doing all those things? Why can you do such a thing? Where is the woman? You are not a real man."' Lesedi explained that there are derogatory Setswana proverbs for men who participate in domestic labour. Since proverbs tend to have long histories, the existence of such phrases illustrates the historical resilience of norms that separate men from household work.

Tshiamo shared:

> I have a partner here, he is not like other partners. He's a person who is willing to help me doing household chores. Sometimes I just stay in the house and rest without doing anything. But in other households you are expected to do everything by yourself. You do the washing, you are alone. But he is able to help me do the washing.

Tshiamo was proud that her partner contributed to household labour in their home, but faced derision from her family for this arrangement. Her mother questioned her partner's masculinity, calling him 'a woman' and insisting he was not a 'real man'. Thus, it appears that individual men choosing to take on a fair proportion of household labour run the risk of ridicule. In Silberschmidt's (2001) study of the disempowerment of men in East Africa, a small proportion of men in the sample assisted their wives with household tasks and were consequently excluded and ridiculed by other men. However, my own participants reported that it is not men but women who deride men for engaging in 'women's work', though perhaps if I had interviewed men I would have discovered a more nuanced picture. The suggestion that women might humiliate men who challenge conventional gender arrangements implies cultural collusion on their part, and raises questions about the attitudes of men themselves, such as whether men would choose to divide labour along non-gendered lines if they were socially supported in doing so.

Lenah, who was married, agreed that a husband's masculinity and competency would be called into question should he participate in 'wifely work': 'They will say who is that man? What kind of a husband is he?' Lenah's own husband did in fact contribute to the cooking and childcare but only when there was nobody else to witness it, indicating that cultural limitations on men's work in the home can undermine a couple's aspirations for more equitable labour division. Connell (2005: 79) contends, 'masculinities constructed in ways that realise the patriarchal dividend, without the tensions or risks of being the frontline troops of patriarchy, are complicit' in perpetuating repressive social structures. In Lenah's case, her husband maintained a pleasant relationship with his wife in part by assisting her with her domestic duties in private. Yet, by appearing outwardly to adhere to customs that preserved male dominance he also continued to benefit from the patriarchal dividend.

Rural and urban participants across a broad age range highlighted the socialization of children into rigid gender roles. Keatlaretse shared that as a child it was made clear to her that she would always do the cooking and cleaning and her brother would not:

> As a woman you cook, you do household chores. Like when I grew up it was me and my elder brother [...] so it was me doing the household chores. [They] were saying my brother is a boy, he doesn't belong in a kitchen [...] So boys grow up knowing that a woman's place is in the kitchen and their place is outside.

Mabedi, living at home with her parents, siblings and child while working towards her master's degree, complained:

> You're expected to clean, to cook, to make, yeah, to cook for everybody in the house. Like my brother can wake up and make his own breakfast and it's fine, but if I wake up and do the same my mother is like, 'What? We haven't eaten', I'm like, 'But he did it first' [...] So I'm expected to cook, I'm also expected to clean, do laundry.

Mabedi resented that her brother 'just does nothing' while she took care of her siblings and parents, cleaned the house, raised her child and studied for her degree. However, her mother was unrelenting in her insistence that these responsibilities were Mabedi's alone, perhaps benefitting from the authority she gained in preserving an oppressive gender order in her household (Kandiyoti, 1988). Emelda asserted that her son could not help with the laundry 'because he is a boy [...] he cannot do it properly so I do it for him'. When I asked why he could not do it properly, she explained that he did not know how to wash clothes and so he might ruin them, and it had never occurred to her to teach him how to wash clothes correctly because boys would not need such skills as men – their domestic requirements would be met by their future wives. Emelda's socialization of her son thus contributed to the cultural reproduction of norms that separate men from the maintenance of their homes.

Shera, an autonomous young urban woman, spoke of her ongoing struggle with the inequitable division of labour in the home. She had recently moved into her partner's place on a temporary basis to trial cohabitation before getting married and starting a family. I interviewed her within the first few weeks of this trial period and she shared the challenges she was facing, in particular from her partner's younger sister, who expected Shera to take responsibility for feeding him:

> So when I get [to his house] the sister is asking me if I brought any food [...] and I said, 'well, I think you should call your brother, why are you asking me?' [...] So anyway, in the morning I was up [...] she's busy with a mop. She's cleaning the house [...] she's telling me, 'oh, you know, [he] really didn't have any food yesterday', and I said, 'your brother is an adult, who works' [...] she's like, 'no, you need to take care of him, and he's even getting thin.'

Shera reflected that she and her partner might have been capable of dividing housework evenly between them had they been left to negotiate their own arrangements without interference. Nonetheless, her efforts to redress the balance of labour in the home were continually undermined by her partner's sister, who lived with him and acted as his servant, expecting Shera to join her in attending to his needs. Previous examples of the patriarchal bargain in action featured older women, who perhaps had more to lose from changing gender relations having accrued certain benefits from a lifetime of obedience (Kandiyoti, 1988). However, in this case a young girl appeared to perceive rewards for compliance, perhaps in the form of financial support or physical protection from her brother, or in approval and validation from her family and community. Such material and social benefits may be sanctioned should she fail to comply with patriarchal norms.

Those participants who expressed resentment towards the inequitable division of household labour nonetheless accepted it as inevitable and challenged it minimally, if at all. Jewkes and Morrell (2010: 7) suggest that hegemonic gender identities are so deeply rooted in social and cultural norms that they generate 'models of behaviour that may be hard for individuals to critique and in which to exercise choice', a useful framework for understanding women's acceptance of gender arrangements that appear not to benefit them. Shera was the exception among my participants in that she actively resisted pressure from her partner, his sister and his friends to comply with their expectations of her 'wifely' subservience. Shera shared another example of the tension she was navigating – upon her return from travelling her partner suggested a celebratory lunch, which he invited his friends to. He anticipated that Shera would prepare the meal:

> I said wait a minute, this man is gonna welcome *me* back by *my* cooking lunch for *him*?! [...] And then my boyfriend says to me: 'Well, I told [my friends] that um, my woman is not um, your ordinary type of woman, so you may come here and starve'. [...] Later, we had a discussion and he said he was managing expectations, but he was also managing the fallout, the judgement, of my being a woman. Or if I'm a suitable woman, you know. [...] And he said: 'Oh but, you should *want* to cook'. I said, 'no no no, I should not want to cook, and I don't want to cook. And what should *you* want to do?' And he said: 'Well I shouldn't want to cook' and I said, 'well, ok, well in that case then I guess we are gonna have a problem'.

Shera recognized that her performance as a homemaker was associated with her perceived suitability as a woman and as a wife and resented the expectation that she would change who she was to win such approval from her partner's friends and family. In the situation described, her partner appeared conflicted. He acknowledged to his friends that Shera was not an 'ordinary' woman, that is, she was not interested in homemaking or caretaking, but seemed somewhat embarrassed by the fact and felt the need to manage his friends' perception of her womanhood, and perhaps of his own masculinity; his use of possessive language ('my woman') was a public display of dominance that was reportedly uncharacteristic of him in private.

While Shera's partner did not insist that she cook, he was perplexed that she had not wanted to cook in the first place. When Shera challenged his assumption that women 'should want to cook' by asking which domestic tasks he 'should want' to carry out he faltered, unable to conceive of any household duty that he might wish to take responsibility for. Shera described him as a liberal intellectual thinker who had always appreciated her independence of thought, and yet, deeply rooted cultural norms in the domestic sphere generated dissonance between them. Such a dynamic is not unexpected in light of the significance of households as 'potent areas for the maintenance or change of our cultural beliefs about who men and women are and how they are (or potentially are not) unequal' (Ridgeway, 2011: 127). Indeed, in Botswana as elsewhere in the world, the family household functions as the epicentre for the construction and maintenance of gender norms. Shera was the only participant to place such emphasis on her need to be respected as an equal partner in all aspects of an intimate relationship. Notwithstanding their long-term intellectual and emotional connection, she was unwilling to commit further to her partner unless they were able to resolve their divergent views on the division of household labour.

Though a minority of my interviewees had never questioned inequitable labour division in the home, many had reflected on its historic context and the impact of recent economic transitions on the status quo. Both rural and urban women largely concluded that the simultaneous obsolescence of traditional male roles and expansion of areas of work for women outside the home had resulted in gender arrangements that were both unfair and impracticable. Tsala and Mpho, both educated urban women in their thirties, explained that historically women and men had separate but mutually beneficial roles to play. However, much of the labour traditionally undertaken by men had been made redundant and had not been replaced with alternatives, nor had it become acceptable for them to assume 'women's work'. Tsala explained:

> I would like to see men getting more involved in the household chores. Because nowadays, really, there is no job for men. Men used to cut wood at home, make fire, fix this and that, build houses, but nowadays we employ people to do all those things, and cook using stoves, there is no cutting firewood and everything. So men literally don't have anything to do at home. All they do is just watch news, watch soccer, and read newspapers.

Mpho thought it was reasonable for women who did not participate in the market economy to take responsibility for household management and childcare. However, she objected to the persistence of those conventional roles as women moved into the workplace: 'Women do the cooking, the cleaning, they take care of the kids. Which is how it was when men were working. But now women also work. But they are still doing the cooking, cleaning, taking care of the kids and running the household, but men are still just only working.' Emelda agreed that in the past: 'The husband was supposed to be the one who is taking care of the woman' so that she could focus solely on the household. The need for 'men's work' in the domestic realm has dwindled with the advent of modern amenities and changing patterns of consumption and has not been replaced with alternatives. Men therefore continue to benefit from women's unpaid labour without contributing what would historically have been their 'fair share', an imbalance that had not escaped the attention of my participants, who nonetheless felt for the most part disempowered to address it. Similarly, Zulu women in South Africa report struggling to manage their domestic obligations now that many of them spend a good proportion of their day working outside of the home in paid employment (Rudwick and Posel, 2015). Failure to redistribute domestic work between men and women following women's transition into formal employment is not exclusive to the sub-Saharan African context. In a study of twenty-two countries of the Global North, the authors concluded that gendered labour division has 'stalled at the door of most households', with only slight increase in the proportion of domestic work done by men since the women entered the formal labour market (Breen and Prince Cooke, 2005). In the contemporary United States the share of household work that falls to women has not changed in proportion to the number of hours they spend in paid labour compared with eras when women were largely excluded from the market economy (Ridgeway, 2011).

Integral to women's role as homemakers is the responsibility for childcare, whether the father of the child(ren) was present or not. Paternal absence is well documented in Botswana and sub-Saharan Africa as a whole (e.g., see Datta, 2011; Kesebonye and Amone-P'Olak, 2021; Maundeni, 2002; Rabie et al., 2020; Thupayagale-Tshweneagae et al., 2012; Trivedi and Bose, 2018), and was considered the norm among my participants. Thato reasoned, 'the wife should be responsible for the kids [...] I know they are both 50/50 responsible [for the conception], but a woman, she takes care of her own kids, and society expects a woman to be responsible.' Similarly, Rudwick and Posel (2015: 294) concluded that 'the assumption that domesticity and childcare are solely the responsibility of women appears to be very resilient' among the Zulu women they interviewed, with very few of their participants viewing the imbalance as 'outdated and gender-biased'. Emelda shared her perception of male parenting: 'It's different because men are not like us, they don't think like us, most of them don't care about their families. We, we cannot eat while your kid is not eating. A man can just eat.'

Given that women were obligated to take on childcare while men were not, most of the mothers in my study parented single-handedly, even if they lived with the father of their children. For Naledi being 'a mother and father at the same time' was a strain, particularly since she was unemployed and had access to few resources in rural Ramotswa where she lived. Tsala's situation was unusual – as a former interpreter she often had to work overseas. Though her husband did not participate in childcare while Tsala was home, he took full responsibility for their children when she travelled: 'When I had to leave my child, my daughter when she was six months, to go to France for a month's course, he stayed with the child. And then when the child was four years old, I had to leave her for one year, to go and study in Reunion Island. He stayed with the kids.' Tsala and her husband had the option of sending their children to stay with female relatives during these periods, a common practice considered beneficial for all parties (Denbow and Thebe, 2006). That the husband chose to remain with his children instead implies that some families view paternal childcare in the mother's absence as a possibility, though this was not indicated by the other participants in my study.

A 'good wife' is expected to be sexually available to her husband on demand, an obligation that many of my participants incorporated into the list of domestic duties expected of women. By custom, 'she must always be ready to gratify his sexual desires' (Schapera, 1940: 94). Since the presentation of *lobola* formerly transferred a woman's reproductive function from her biological family to her husband's family, it was often interpreted as giving the husband total sexual control over his wife: 'these women can't stop us', 'we have given *bogadi* for them, and so we are entitled to make use of their bodies' (Schapera, 1940: 63).[1] Despite significant advancements in women's autonomy in the decades since Schapera's observations, the perception of women's bodies as property, particularly those who are married, has persevered (Phorano et al., 2005).

As discussed in the introductory chapter, marital rape is not recognized as a crime in either of Botswana's legal systems. Women from all backgrounds in my study spoke of the expectation of wives to provide sex on demand, and many seemed resigned to it. Thato shrugged as she told me, 'the man will be wanting whatever he wants'. Maatla believed that women ought not undertake manual labour because they needed to conserve energy for sex: 'if she has a man at home, he wants to be satisfied, he wants bedroom work to be done, and if you're tired then how else are you going to deliver?' While 'bedroom work' might merely be a euphemism for sexual activity, it is noteworthy that Maatla used the term 'work' to express sex from a woman's perspective. The construction of sex as a labour requirement undermines women's own sexuality. Indeed, none of the participants indicated that a woman might enjoy sex. Rapoo (2013: 17) has shown that Botswana culture constructs sexual pleasure as a 'luxury reserved for men'. The participants who mentioned sex emphasized it as one chore in a list of many, a consensus shared by women from all backgrounds. Mpho recounted the instructions married women provided to new brides: 'You know, as soon as he um, whatever he wants to do you should do, when he wants to make love you should make love.' This follows from Schapera's historic finding that upon marriage female relatives would advise the new wife 'to submit to her husband's attentions whenever he wants her', for 'it is her duty to afford him carnal satisfaction' (Schapera, 1940: 162), indicating the resilience of such norms.

Women in the market economy

Rural women in Botswana suffer disproportionately from poverty (Akinsola and Popovich, 2002), and this was reflected in my sample; of the seven who were unemployed, five were rural women, and all five women in my study who worked low-income jobs in the service industry were from rural areas. Among the ten women who were unemployed or worked in low-paid roles, only one was married and had access to financial support from her husband. All struggled to make ends meet and lived in impoverished conditions. All my participants either worked outside of the home in formal employment or wanted to. While most carried an onerous weight of labour as homemakers, paid work was desirable and/or necessary. For rural mothers like Naledi, Elizabeth and Khana, survival was the only reason a woman would enter the market economy. Alternative considerations such as vocational interest, personal satisfaction or socioeconomic status were absent from their conceptualizations of paid work. Naledi believed that women did not belong in the workplace but conceded that formal employment was essential for survival in the absence of a breadwinner in the home: 'Here women are working [...] we work because we know that life is expensive.' Similarly, mother of three, Elizabeth, who held a very low-paid job as a school bus driver, thought women should be mothers and wives above all else, but 'being a working mother is good because [...] if you are not working you suffer, you don't know where to find the money.' Elizabeth was married, but her husband's income was insufficient to support their family of five.

Single mother Khana's story supports the view that economic need was the primary driver of rural women seeking work. She described the extent of her search for business across Africa to raise money for her daughter's school fees, and the emotional strain it caused her:

> In Botswana we are struggling as ladies. [...] That's the struggle I had most, the bad times that I had. Because imagine when you leave a child of eleven years old. You go as far as Zambia, maybe 1000km from home. Not knowing what can happen to your child when you're not there. Maybe the house can be burnt and your daughter can be burnt [...] maybe people can get inside the house and rape her.

Khana had to leave her young daughter at home by herself while she travelled abroad for work so she could fund her daughter's secondary education. As noted earlier, free education is available in Botswana. However, aware of the poor quality of teaching in government schools, many families prefer to send their children to private schools which meet international standards of education. Several of my participants with children of their own, and those who took care of others' children, opted to sacrifice basic necessities to pay for private education. Khana's story is indicative of the lengths some women feel compelled to take to provide quality education for their children. For Khana, paying for her daughter's private education was an investment in her own future. She was conscious that if her daughter received a good education she was more likely to find financial security through work, and thus be in a position to support Khana in her advancing years.

According to conventional gender arrangements, men would provide financially for their families while women managed the home and cared for the children and other family members. Yet, women's trust in this form of support was breaking down, even for those who did have working husbands or partners. Reneilwe, who was twenty-five, pointed out, '[in] modern days they say women also have to work. Of which, long ago, women were not allowed to work. They trusted the men. Of which, as youngsters we don't trust. I won't say: "Ah, okay, I have this boyfriend, I trust that he will take care of me". I don't trust he'll continue taking care of me.' Reneilwe expressed conservative views throughout her interview, emphatically endorsing patriarchal values and codes of behaviour. Yet, she did not feel confident that the men she dated, or a future husband, would support her financially. She sought formal employment as a preventative measure against an anticipated failure of men to provide.

Kandiyoti (1988: 277) reveals that in sub-Saharan Africa women often find themselves lacking financial assistance from their husbands and as such, they 'have very little to gain and a lot to lose by becoming totally dependent' on them. While Reneilwe idealized the position of subservient wife, as mentioned earlier, she did not want to rely solely on a husband to meet her material needs and resented the idea of 'always asking for five pula, toiletries' (five pula is approximately £0.33). Reneilwe was able to be selective about the patriarchal customs she chose to adhere to and which she chose to reject, preserving some aspects of the hegemonic gender order while securing financial independence for herself.

The rural participants generally articulated the need for formal employment as little more than a means for survival, but Kesegofetse, a magistrate, was unique among my rural cohort in expressing vocational passion. When I asked her what she wanted for her life, she exclaimed unhesitatingly, 'to be a judge!' This was at odds with most of my rural participants, who framed their answer in terms of intimate relationship goals and did not list a career as an aspiration for their lives. My urban participants, on the other hand, frequently spoke of their work in terms other than economic need. Neo shared animatedly her dedication to her work in Botswana's economic development sector, and Pono exclaimed, 'we want to be up there in the offices, holding high positions!'

Akhu, a saxophone performer, had left a steady job as a teacher to begin her own music school. Though her career transition was motivated by her love for music, it was her economic stability that enabled her to take the financial risk of starting her own business. She was nervous that the music school might not be successful, but her fears were personal, not financial. Similarly, Basadi, a design researcher, was searching for a new job that would allow her more creative autonomy, even if it paid less than her current role.

For Thato, a married urban teacher, her job was less about personal fulfilment and more about financial independence. However, unlike the rural participants, she linked financial independence with freedom rather than with survival: 'working gives [a woman] freedom to do whatever she wants […] she doesn't have to depend on her husband or on the boyfriend […] when she wants to buy something she goes out and buys'. Although Thato was married, she preferred to have a separate income that she was free to spend as she wished. Thato expressed the belief that women should have 'much more freedom' in all realms, and that men and women should have equal access to opportunities that would allow them to meet their own material needs. For Thato, economic self-sufficiency was an important element of the wider context of gender equality concerns.

The meanings attributed to formal employment largely diverged between settlement types. The significant difference in economic opportunity between urban and rural areas could account for the disparate priorities of those who lived in villages and those who lived in the city. Economic development in Botswana has been uneven; 10.5 per cent of the rural population live in poverty compared with 1.7 per cent in cities and towns (Magombeyi and Odhiambo, 2017). People in rural areas continue to face barriers to accessing education, and literacy rates are lower than those in urban areas (Denbow and Thebe, 2006). There are few primary schools in remote villages. As such, parents must often send their children to expensive boarding schools in the cities. This challenge to education access is compounded by the need to keep children at home where their labour in the rural subsistence economy is invaluable (Denbow and Thebe, 2006). Thus, women living in cities are more likely to be financially stable and better educated, which could account for their awareness of the broader political implications of paid labour as well as their freedom to prioritize issues that go beyond economic survival.

The informal sector in Botswana encompasses economic activities that are unregistered and unregulated, small, casual and often temporary or mobile, such as street vending or hawking. Though the transient nature of informal employment makes reliable prevalence data difficult to ascertain, it is estimated that nearly 75 per cent of women (and over 60 per cent of men) work in the informal sector in Africa as a whole (Government of Botswana, 2020). In the formal sector, women are disproportionately employed in lower-paying fields such as retail, factory work, catering, service, education and administration (Van Klaveren et al., 2009). Fourteen of the women I interviewed worked in these fields, seven of whom were teachers or lecturers and three of whom worked in other roles within schools. Six of my participants worked in alternative sectors (design, law, medicine, research, finance and ICT), eight were not formally employed and two were students.[2]

Kevane (2014: 117) points out that in sub-Saharan Africa it is not usually chiefs, heads of state or authority figures in general who demarcate types of work by gender. Rather, the gendered division of labour 'seems to be sustained by informal norms operating at the level of households and communities'. This is the case in Botswana, where there are no legal restrictions on the work that women (and men) can do. Informal gender segregation of occupations, and of job roles or specialisms within occupations, continues to be a major factor in shaping the labour market worldwide, including in affluent countries. In the United States, for example, the labour force is overwhelmingly segregated along gender lines similar to those that have materialized in Botswana's emergent market economy; in the United States the job types and roles 'in which men and women are concentrated often appear to reflect cultural beliefs about gender, including status differences between the sexes and stereotypic assumptions about each sex's specialized skills' (Ridgeway, 2011: 97). In the United States and other wealthy industrialized nations women are more often found in roles that reflect assumptions about their nature as inherently communal, interpersonal and nurturing, such as service jobs and roles with less authority. Men, in contrast, tend to be found in work that reflects the agentic skills and attributes they are assumed to possess, including instrumental competence and assertiveness, such as manual labour and more senior positions (Ridgeway, 2011). The economic impact of gendered segregation in employment is profound; 'the more women predominate in a job, the less it pays' (Ridgeway, 2011: 98).

Lenah suggested that the gendered division of labour in Botswana stems from the perception of women as caregivers: 'Women are expected to be home taking care of kids [...] most of the teachers here are women. Because of what? Of babysitting [...] Because of that perception of a woman taking care of the kids.' Other interviewees attributed the gendered division of labour to physical differences. These participants argued that women's bodies render them unsuitable for manual labour, that 'women need lighter jobs because they are fragile' (Maatla). Maatla elaborated that women tend to become 'nurses, teachers, cleaners [...] jobs that are much lighter to handle than [those] men have'. In total five of the participants perceived women as physically weak, thus requiring 'lighter' jobs. Relatedly, Reneilwe pointed to the discomfort of menstruation as a factor in the gendering of work: 'When you are on your cycle, menstrual cycle. You know when, there are some times when you feel like, just moody. And you know that when you bend too much it's going to hurt, it's going to be painful.' The perception of women as unsuitable for certain positions is likely to be a contributing factor in the high unemployment rates among women. The limited view of women's physical capacity is peculiar in the historic context of Botswana's agricultural subsistence economy, in which women typically undertook heavy manual work such as ploughing fields, pounding grain and carrying water (Schapera, 1938). In this context, it could be reasoned that the perception of women as physically weak is indicative of the penetration of new cultural norms through processes of colonization and globalization, discussed further in the next chapter.

While gender at work was not an area that I covered explicitly in my interviews, most of the participants spoke unprompted about gender arrangements in the workplace. A minority shared positive reflections on the status of women at work. Kesegofetse pointed out, 'some [women] have even taken senior positions where they are working', and in the rural courthouse where she worked there were more female magistrates than when she joined several years prior. Lesedi was confident that there was equality in treatment and pay at the school where she taught: 'The male people, I am just at par with them, regardless of me being a woman, we are just the same. We get the same pay for as long as we are having the same job.' Nevertheless, her positive view was tempered by her assertion that women are generally 'not penetrating as far as the job world is concerned. You will find very few women in high positions', a view most of the participants agreed with. Neo asserted, 'when you look at, say, the amount of women that are in positions of leadership, CEOs, that's still really a small percentage.' Tumelo described the hierarchy of positions at the public land board where she worked: 'The sub land boards, they are all headed by men. And then their deputies are men except for two. And then middle management, let me see, we are nearly equally balanced there.' Tsala reported a similar structure in private sector jobs, where 'the higher you go in the work market, you will find that the society will prefer a man over a woman. And also if there is a woman for that post, women are normally paid less than their male counterparts'.

A number of the women I interviewed provided examples of sexism in the workplace that manifested in pay gaps, lack of respect, sexual harassment and the glass ceiling,[3] expressing frustration with the gendered hierarchy in the formal labour environment. Reneilwe claimed, 'men rule everything. Wherever you go you will find that man is on the top. Women in an organization they have to follow that man. That man is the boss [...] maybe 90 per cent of men in Botswana, they are the boss, top leaders in everything.' Sefela agreed, 'men are always above women, and women come after.' The enduring cultural construction of men as 'natural' leaders limits women's penetration in senior positions. Setswana proverbs support the superiority of male leaders and explicitly undermine women's leadership capabilities. For example: 'a team of oxen is never led by females, otherwise the oxen will fall into a ditch – men are natural leaders' (*ga di nke ke etelelwa ke manamagadi pele, di ka wela selomo – banna ke baeteledipele ka tholego*) (UNDP, 2012: 11). In this popular analogy, women leaders are portrayed as a liability. Another version loosely translates as 'cows will never lead the herd' (*ga nke di etelelwa pel eke managadi*) (Bauer, 2010: 62). Proverbs like this preserve the widespread notion that women are weak leaders, encouraging their exclusion from senior positions, and damage women's own self-confidence, discouraging them from seeking leadership positions in the first place (UNDP, 2012).

A multitude of interpersonal, structural, organizational and cultural barriers to the advancement of women in leadership positions are evident to different degrees throughout sub-Saharan Africa, including girlhood socialization; lack of opportunities for education, skills training and professional qualifications; male dominance and lack of support from husbands; expectations of role fulfilment as wives and mothers; perceptions of women as less competent and too emotional; and recruitment and promotion procedures within organizations (Nkomo and Ngambi, 2009). In the Global North, too, women are underrepresented at all levels of leadership. In the United States, women of colour, lesbian, bisexual, and transgender women (Hill et al., 2016) and women with disabilities (UN, 2018) are excluded from leadership roles at higher rates than the average for all women, and only eight of the United Kingdom's top 100 companies were led by women in 2021, the highest number since records were first published in 1999 (Vinnicombe et al., 2021).

For the minority of women who are able to secure a senior role within their organization, there is a risk of social fallout with colleagues and family. Basadi faced interpersonal problems at work as a result of her success:

> You have to be respectful. You have to show a lot of humility [as a woman]. Okay so one of the reasons I don't want to work here. I interned here for a while before studying my master's degree. And one of the big issues in the office was that if you're very serious about your work, if you try to do your work well and on time and you care about the quality, and you, you know you put a lot of effort into it, it's seen as being very competitive [...] And our society, I think Setswana culture for sure, doesn't appreciate that. And so when you're seen to be competitive, especially if you're a woman, that's seen as a negative thing.

In a culture that is expressed through communal social structures (Denbow and Thebe, 2006; Schapera, 1938), it follows that the perception of individual competitiveness might create tension. However, the effects are both more pronounced and more detrimental for women – being ambitious, competitive or driven is seen as antithetical to the humility and self-sacrifice considered essential for womanhood. Akhu had observed similar tensions in the school where she worked for many years. She explained: 'if the school head is a woman, or the deputy school head is a woman, usually some male teachers will not really give her the respect she deserves.' Though education is considered a suitable arena for women, women in senior roles might yet face challenges to their authority from their male juniors.

Taemane lamented that women finding any measure of success in the workplace leads to 'fights or conflicts' with their male partners: 'He wants to challenge you [because] he thinks you've got a better job than him.' Mpho agreed that there could be 'tension, of she's bringing more money into the situation than he is'. She expanded: 'There's still a stigma that you know, a woman, you can work but [...] once you get a man you have to sort of be on par, or just below par, or way below par.' Many women feel compelled to leave formal employment on marriage regardless of whether their families would benefit from their income or if they found value or enjoyment in their work. In some communities it was deemed inappropriate for a married woman to earn money, particularly if she earned more than her husband. Shera had found that a married woman was perceived as less threatening than a single woman in the workplace, because it was generally understood that she would not compete for higher positions; married women were a 'stable entity'. Such a view reveals the assumption that women will minimize their career ambitions to avoid role conflict with their husbands or male partners. Whether this strategy represents agency or powerlessness is unclear; women's balancing of their vocational preferences with their husbands' self-image is an important area for further study. Denbow and Thebe (2006: 153) suggest that Batswana men prefer to partner with a woman who has less 'education, status, salary, or power' than they, 'thus keeping the relative relations of power within the family intact'. Indeed, 'male dominance, unsupportive husbands, and the inferiority complex of their husbands' have been shown to present significant barriers to women's career advancement in other parts of southern Africa and East Africa (Nkomo and Ngambi, 2009).

An ambitious young woman, Pamela had studied for a vocational qualification and eagerly anticipated finding a job in her field. She was angered and discouraged to be sexually propositioned following a successful interview:

> I went for an interview for a job. Accounts assistant. [...] and I'm told, 'come tomorrow to sign the contract papers and start work'. And then the boss, the big boss, calls me to the office. When I get there, he offers me sex. He's like, 'if you sleep with me I'll bump up your salary' [...] And then I didn't get hired because I didn't sleep with the boss man. He didn't take me seriously. He didn't take my education seriously. I mean I went to school for years for that degree, and he didn't take that into

account […] I didn't like that. I didn't like being objectified like that, and it made me angry.

Pamela's story demonstrates the challenges and risks facing young women attempting to enter the male-dominated market economy. Even for women with the opportunities and resources to pursue a career, their career trajectories are vulnerable to disruption by harmful gendered attitudes and behaviours. While most of the women I interviewed wanted or needed to work, whether primarily for economic stability or for personal satisfaction, they faced a myriad of obstacles in securing the jobs they desired and in achieving respect and stability in their positions.

Serving kin and the community

Kinship networks have long been a source of support for individuals across much of Africa, where the impact of financial, emotional and practical difficulties can be alleviated through various forms of assistance from members of the extended kin group (Harper and Seekings, 2010). In Botswana such support manifests in numerous ways. For example, urban kin send cash to rural family members in times of need; rural kin send food they have produced to those struggling in the towns, or take them back into the village homestead; communities pull together to assist members with tasks such as thatching roofs, building and farming; and households who do not have the financial or practical resources to care for their offspring often send one or more children to live with other family members, either permanently or on a temporary basis (Mupedziswa and Ntseane, 2013). Women must 'get involved with the community, take care of the neighbours, take care of people in the society, share the little that you have' (Tsala). Reciprocity is a fundamental principle of kin support networks (Harper and Seekings, 2010). However, for the most part, my participants perceived this system of resource and labour exchange as a tremendous burden rather than as mutually beneficial support.

Several interviewees spoke about their experiences of taking care of other women's children. For some women this meant bringing children to live with them on a permanent basis – often younger siblings, nieces or nephews. Others made regular financial contributions to cover food, school fees and transport. Malisa lamented the sacrifices she had to make to care for her younger sister:

> When things were not going well at home I took her in and stayed with her. I paid for her school fees until she finished, then she went to varsity. I had no choice, it was not my responsibility, but I had no choice but to do it. And, you know you, you tend to really put some of your plans on hold, you know, because you have to help somebody else.

Though kinship provision is a long-standing and widespread practice, Malisa rejected the view that she was socially obligated to support her sister financially and practically, feeling that the personal cost to her was too high. Her resistance remained internal, she felt compelled by her family to take on the additional responsibility and did not feel empowered to refuse. Her sense of loss was apparent as she went on to describe the things she had to relinquish so that she could cover her sister's needs, including her professional development. While 'acknowledging responsibilities toward one's kin' functions as a basic organizing principle of many African societies (Harper and Seekings, 2010: 27), for some of my participants their kinship obligations generated profound resentment.

Lenah, an urban teacher with three children of her own, assisted her brother's family by bringing two of his children to live with her. Her brother and his wife were struggling under the strain of caring for multiple children, and Lenah was concerned that some of those children would end up 'living with, you know how extended our families are, usually an aunt of an aunt', far from their parents, if she did not step in to help. Despite her own limited resources, Lenah assumed full financial and caregiving responsibility for two of her nieces. Lenah could barely afford two additional children and the extra bodies overcrowded an already cramped home, yet, like Malisa, she felt she had no choice. Thato, also an urban teacher and mother of one, regretted the sacrifices she had made to support her nephews. Once she had covered her own child's financial needs, her remaining funds went towards 'transporting my sister's kid to school. Then there will be nothing left for me'. In a similarly disheartened tone, Naledi, rural unemployed mother of one, complained of spending all her time caring for her sister's baby. She described a typical day: 'First I prepare his porridge, and then make sure the milk is ready, then clean the house and wait for him to wake up. Then I will just be sitting with him the whole day.' Naledi needed employment but having a young child and an infant to care for limited her freedom of movement to go out and find work.

My participants struggled with their social obligations to their extended families, which they experienced as a strain on their limited financial and emotional resources in addition to reducing the time available to them for their own pursuits. The nature of complaints about kin obligations reflects the findings of Aboderin's (2003) research into the decline of material support for older family members in Ghana. Ghana is comparable with Botswana in several ways: Traditional Ghanaian society was structured on kinship and rooted in subsistence agriculture; it gained independence from the United Kingdom in 1957 and is now a democratic nation state; its people are predominantly Christian; the advent of colonial rule, formal education and the cash economy have all altered aspects of Ghanaian life, and Ghanaians are experiencing widespread unemployment and rising living costs (Aboderin, 2003). Aboderin posits two reasons for the decline of kin support. The first, emerging individualism and the weakening of traditional family structures undermining belief in the value and necessity of supporting one's kin. The second and most significant, new standards of living and increased materialism have made everyday life more expensive. As such, many Ghanaians no longer feel that they can spare enough for their elders' upkeep (Aboderin, 2003). While Aboderin's study is focused on material assistance for older people, I argue that her findings reflect my participants' experiences of supporting family members of all generations, particularly as many of my interviewees' complaints were rooted in the economic hardship and material sacrifices required of them to support their kin. Pamela, as the only girl in the family, found that the duty of caring for her four siblings fell to her in the absence of her parents, though she was unemployed at the time and had a child of her own: 'Well, I'm the only girl. And I have, you know, my Mum died. As you know. Four years ago. And then when she died my Dad was in jail. So I had to take care of my brothers.' It is commonly expected that women of the family or community raise children whose parents have died or left (Malinga and Ntshwarang, 2011). For Pamela, raising her brothers was a constant battle, one that she had not asked for. Her brothers did not accept her parental authority and treated her poorly.

Tshiamo shared that as the first-born female child it had been her duty to act 'like a mother' to her siblings when she was younger, 'washing nappies [...] cook for them, bath them, do anything that a mother could do for a child'. As she got older these obligations continued; for example, she paid the school fees for her youngest sibling. One of Tshiamo's children lived with her paternal grandmother, whom she also supported financially. Although there was some ambiguity in Tshiamo's description of the situation, the context she gave suggested that the child had been offered to provide practical support for an ageing woman. Tshiamo's kinship caregiving obligations had taken many forms over the years – in her youth she provided practical assistance, later financial support, eventually sending a child of her own to help the family. Whether or not Tshiamo also benefitted from having her child live with her grandmother was unclear. Sending a child to live with close relatives or extended kin is often to the benefit of the child's parent(s), since it is usually done in cases where they cannot afford the child's upkeep (Aboderin, 2003; Harper and Seekings, 2010; Mupedziswa and Ntseane, 2013). However, in this case Tshiamo was also providing financially for her grandmother, seemingly negating any financial benefit for Tshiamo. Certainly, Tshiamo did not give the impression that the aid she extended to her kin had been reciprocated at any stage in her life.

Most of the participants who spoke about kin support offered narratives that implied a lack of reciprocity to their efforts, focusing instead on the burdens of their kinship obligations. This negative framework might have resulted from the tendency for women to use interviews as an outlet for grievances that they would not otherwise have the opportunity to express (LeVine, 1979). However, research into claims on and obligations to kin in South Africa suggests that young Black adults experience their kinship ties as obligations more frequently than as sources of support (Harper and Seekings, 2010). It appears to be the case that the 'persistent ideology of extended obligations (one *should* support one's kin, including more distant kin)' is at odds with 'the reality of restricted claims (in practice, one can only make claims on immediate kin)' (Harper and Seekings, 2010: 24). Additionally, young Black adults might be reluctant to ask for financial support out of feelings of pride and anxiousness around taking money (Harper and Seekings, 2010). It is possible that such dynamics were at play among my participants, though they were older than the people in Harper and Seeking's study. For some of my participants, there was simply nobody from whom they could lay claim to reciprocal support due to the limited resources of other family members.

While many of the women in my sample spoke of providing or receiving practical and financial support in relation to children or siblings, they were also subject to demands on their resources from adults in their kin network. Keatlaretse, unemployed urban mother of one, cared for her sister's children, and when she had been employed she had also supported her mother financially. When her aunt was diagnosed with cancer during the same period, Keatlaretse took her to all of her medical appointments and provided money and food as well as practical care. The burden of so much responsibility was unsustainable, causing stress and exhaustion which affected her health and her performance at work. Ultimately she lost her job, leaving her with no means to continue supporting those who depended on her. She believed the weight of her obligations to her family cost her the opportunity to secure stability for herself through land purchase, particularly since she no longer had an income of her own. She reflected:

> It is expected for us to, when you start working and all that, give your mum money [...] And those things are a setback for a lot of us. [...] when I started working I started to be more like the father now, helping her [financially]. And if not for those things, maybe, I believe I would be having my own place now. That's the life I would have wanted [...] My sisters left their kids here, I also make sure the kids are okay, eat, if they are not well take them to the doctor and all those things, for their sake [...] So I think other than that I think by now my life would be different and better as well.

It is noteworthy that Keatlaretse associated her financial support of the family with the customarily masculine role of breadwinner – 'like the father'. Her gendered conceptualization of material provision indicates the persistence of the cultural construction of men as providers despite high rates of female-headed households and single motherhood. Like Keatlaretse, Khana lamented that although she would have liked to build her own home, her disposable income had always been reserved for her mother. She thought it unlikely at this stage in her life that she would be able to fulfil her primary ambition of becoming a homeowner.

Perhaps unsurprisingly, where extended familial provision was multi-directional it was experienced as a positive, rewarding exchange rather than as an unwelcome responsibility. Emelda had been both giver and beneficiary of the familial support women are often obligated to provide, and as such she welcomed the custom. Her sister helped to send Emelda's son to school when Emelda was not earning enough:

> She said, 'no, you bring the kid here […] I will go in with the kid in the morning'. And I said, 'and what about the food?' […] she said, 'no, this kid is my kid, so he's going to eat what I eat, I'm going to help you with the transport money' […] so my sister is the one who made my life easier.

Once Emelda began earning money, she was able to return the favour: 'I just call and say this month I'm the one who is buying some chips for the kids for school, I'll be taking care of the lunchbox'. For Emelda, the kinship support network was continuous and cyclical, each sister helping the other as and when they were able to.

Laone shared that she was being supported by a female friend, who would 'come to her house with bags of groceries' if she was struggling for money. Elizabeth received similar help from her aunts: 'Sometimes when I say I don't have something to eat, they say, "no, you don't have money, just come and take meat, come and take something".' The cultural expectation that those with resources, however limited, ought to provide for those in need, offered a safety net that some of my participants benefited from, including Tumelo and Lesedi. Tumelo's child lived with her mother who was viewed as a more reliable source of childcare than a nanny, with Tumelo and her partner visiting him 'at month end'. This system was effective for Tumelo who was able to pursue her career without the burden of childcare. Similarly, Lesedi's youngest daughter lived with Lesedi's mother, an arrangement so common that Lesedi had never considered an alternative: 'I have never thought of taking my kid for as long as my mother is still there, I have no problem just, I just leave them at home.' Although Lesedi's mother was looking after Lesedi's child full-time, Lesedi was not without kin obligations of her own: 'I'm just doing my duty as a daughter to buy her some things […] so I'll buy clothes for my mum, for my daughter, even for my sister's kids if I have money […] the one is using a bus to go to school, so sometimes if I have money […] I will pay for [their] bus fare.' The female network of kinship support was crucial in ensuring that women with few resources were able to meet their basic needs,[4] though became problematic when the resource strain on those providing for others was too great and the personal costs too high. Nonetheless, none of the women in my study who spoke about providing kin support indicated that it was optional in the context of sociocultural expectations.

In addition to the extended childcare and economic assistance described above, women are obligated to run errands for their family and the wider community on a daily basis. Neo, an urban woman who worked full-time, described feeling overextended by her family's demands: 'So this person calls, "can you pick up the kids for me?" Okay I'll do it. "Can you do this?" Okay I'll do it. It was just yes yes yes to everything. And then I was giving from the wrong place and yeah, then it felt like a sacrifice.' Mpho described how seniority is implicated in community expectations of labour provision: 'I think here because of the way family structure is, it's okay for, you know, an aunt or a second uncle to call you and be like, "Can you do this?" As long as you know, you're younger than them, you have to do it.'

Some of my interviewees indicated that women's fulfilment of their myriad obligations was only considered sufficient if duties were completed to a certain standard. Mpho elaborated:

> I feel like women's work is just never done. Just constantly, it's kids, it's work, it's family, I think a lot of women are successful at that. And that's what society would judge as successful. But it's also a very very harsh judgement. So if you're not doing it well enough, or to their standards, you know, God forbid if you, I don't know, are working all day, and then you have a family function in the evening, so you just decide to buy cakes, instead of make cakes. You know that's a judgement. You provided the cakes but you're being judged because you didn't make them. And a woman, you know, should cook. Or you've hired a caterer instead of making [food], and you know everybody's like, 'oh, you're so lazy, that woman is so lazy'. But you know, when you think of all the things she's doing from day-to-day, you know the fact that she even had the time to call somebody to cater is you know, is a lot.

Mpho's story illustrates how women's performance of gendered responsibilities was judged by an elevated standard of femininity. Striving to meet such standards demanded extensive time and energy resource, and contributed to feelings of stress, overwhelm and inadequacy among the women I interviewed.

Conforming to hegemonic femininity

Sennott and Mojola's (2017: 8) study of transition to respectable womanhood in rural South Africa found that 'behaving well' (*mahanyelo ya kahle*) as a woman meant 'to adhere to socio-cultural norms for ideal – or acquiescent – femininity', including 'talking well, respecting others, being humble, avoiding gossip, and taking care of others'. For my participants, too, the performance of hegemonic femininity was an expectation, and often a burden, that permeated all realms of a woman's life. Traditionally it was considered that women 'must ideally be hard-working and obedient, modest, chaste, and generally well behaved' (Schapera, 1938: 128), 'industrious, meek and modest' (Schapera, 1940: 34). My interviews suggested this was still very much thought to be the case, with ideal femininity described in terms of compliance, subservience, respect and emotionality. When asked what a 'good Motswana woman' would be like, my participants painted an image of somebody 'who is humble, who is diligent' (Tshepiso); 'obedient' (Lesedi); 'somebody who has got good morals and principles' (Ona); 'accommodating' and 'easy to talk to, able to comfort you' (Taemane); 'able to advise' (Sefela); 'giving' and 'compassionate' (Laone); 'emotional' (Keeya); 'disciplined', 'patient' and 'caring' (Beth); 'know other people's needs' (Naledi); 'responsible' (Thato) and 'loving' (Maatla). Some of the women I spoke to expressed a personal belief that women ought to demonstrate such attributes, others had no personal expectation of women to do so, but acknowledged that feminine characteristics were an important part of cultural expectations of womanhood and were necessary for social approval. Obedience was an oft-cited trait in the 'good' Motswana woman: 'A good Motswana woman, I will say they want somebody who is obedient, and yeah, I think obedience is the key thing [...] obedience is an ideal woman' (Lesedi). Women were to be obedient first of all to men, and secondly to their female seniors. Sefela and Tshepiso also spoke of obedience to a Christian God as a virtuous trait: 'Somebody who follows the rules of God, who is aligned to Christianity and listens and obeys' (Sefela), 'who knows the Word and follows' (Tshepiso).

'Respectfulness' was repeated several times in answer to the questions, 'what qualities do you value in a woman?' and 'what is expected of a Motswana woman?' Sennott and Mojola (2017) reported similar findings in rural South

Africa, where respecting others was an important part of 'behaving well'. My interpretation of the use of 'respect' in the Botswana context, particularly in discussions about gender, is that the meaning is aligned more closely with humility or deference than with admiration, as the term may otherwise be used to connote. Malisa asserted that women must be respectful, otherwise 'people will label you' as a lesser woman. She stated that when her son gets married and his wife comes to live in her home, respectfulness on her part would be key to household harmony: 'If the wife does not have respect, was not brought up properly, I don't think there will be peace in the house.' Malisa expected her son's future wife to show deferential respect to her son and to her as the senior woman of the household. Such respect would manifest in willingness to cook, clean and carry out other domestic tasks; in putting the needs of other household members before her own and in accepting the requirements and demands of her husband and mother-in-law without questioning or complaining. Respectfulness was also expected from women outside of the home; for example, in the formal work environment. Malisa explained that for women, 'when it comes to issues of promotion people say, "oh, not this one, she doesn't [show] respect"'. However, while women are expected to be respectful to men and to their female seniors, they are unlikely to be respected themselves: 'Society they will just undermine you because you are a woman. Men generally have respect, they are respected [...] a man is a man, and if you are a woman, you are a woman.' Generalized lack of respect for women, and particularly young unmarried women, has a detrimental effect on self-confidence which in turn can lead to mental health problems, reduced assertiveness, limited professional advancement and a host of other negative consequences.

The requirement of women to be deferential is problematic for those who seek to assert their personal needs or voice an independent viewpoint; in making themselves heard, they risk characterization as 'masculine' which makes them less desirable to men and undermines their acceptance as women in the community. In the United States it has been shown that 'the most undesirable traits in women are those like domineering and arrogant that violate the cultural presumption of women's subordinate status' (Ridgeway, 2011: 59), a pattern my participants noted in the Botswana context. Assertiveness was another proscribed trait in women, a trend repeatedly evidenced in research from around the world (Bossuyt and Van Kenhove, 2018). Keatlaretse found that asserting her principles was a problem because 'those things chase men away'. In instances where she had attempted to be assertive with her ideas, she shared that people 'end up thinking that you are now trying to be the man'. She elaborated: 'They believe that, I don't know, this belief of a woman, you know, demanding this and that. In our culture it's more like a man is supposed to be giving [the ideas].' Neo was among the participants who reported a personal aversion to self-assured women, stating that she would dislike any woman who 'tried to be like a man. Yeah, sort of um, over-powering'. Women are not encouraged to express their opinions or take initiative, however useful, insightful or significant their ideas might be: 'No matter how good you do, there will always be that clause to say, "after all, she's just a woman, what can she tell you?"'.

In the context of patriarchy women's voices are intrinsically less valuable than men's voices, and those who speak out may be reproached, particularly if what they have to say challenges cultural or gendered norms within the family, community and the workplace. Keeya elucidated that women should be:

> Wishy-washy kind of. Because you must be pleasant and you must be liked and you must just, don't ruffle feathers. Just, you know, whatever's going on, just see how you can fit yourself in there nicely. And you know, in a home, if your husband wants things a certain way just, you know, just comply and make him happy, don't be too assertive.

Keeya was personally conflicted – though she wanted to present herself authentically, social expectations of her to be compliant and self-sacrificing limited her ability to do so. She admired women who were self-assured and who stood by their principles, but she struggled to uphold these values for herself, ever conscious that women are 'supposed to be the flexible ones'. As such, she harboured a 'fear of asserting' herself and a 'fear of saying no'.

Mpho spoke of the difficulties faced by women who asserted their needs in relationships with men, and the judgement they faced from men and from other women in doing so:

> I think, men in our society have always been like, 'You are the king, you are the lion [...] and your woman, no matter what, is, you know, submissive to you' [...] like if a woman is strong and stands up to her man and says, 'I'm

not gonna quit my job [on marriage], I'm not gonna do that', you know, she's hearing twitter from women who are saying, you know, 'She's such a horrible wife', and you know, and then men would be saying that, 'You can't have a wife you can't control'.

Indeed, many global studies have shown that women acting with assertiveness receive a negative response from their peers, and as such women are less likely to take a stand than men (Bossuyt and Van Kenhove, 2018). Women who are strong, assertive and stand their ground in disputes are construed as problematic because their behaviour is seen to undermine male authority, the cornerstone of a patriarchal gender order. Mpho's example demonstrates a social process in which women who assert themselves in their relationships with men are vilified as offensive and out of control, preserving the appearance of male dominance and keeping gendered power dynamics visibly intact. Mpho admitted that despite valuing independent women on a personal level and living an autonomous lifestyle of her own, when in groups of women she had a tendency to participate in social policing and regulation of the behaviour of those who did not confirm to the ideals of submissive femininity: 'We've caught ourselves being like, "oh what is she gonna do when she gets married?" [...] because, you know, nobody wants a bride who doesn't know her customs, who doesn't know how to be a Motswana woman'. Contradictory notions of womanhood coexisted in Mpho's mind; perhaps her worldview was shaped in part by her extensive international travel. I discuss the global influences on Mpho's interpretation of cultural norms further in the next chapter.

Mabedi did not view herself as a particularly feminine person by nature and struggled to conform to essentialist notions of womanhood, resulting in identity conflict that she found to be a daily challenge within her social and familial groups. Here she gave an example of instinctive behaviour that was seen to be problematic, which she sought to modify by imitating the socially acceptable behaviour of her female friends:

When you're a woman and you're not very emotional, they call you a man. It's like, 'you're such a man', because they expect you to act in a certain way [...] When you see a baby, you know women [...] they go 'aww'. And I don't get that reaction, so they're always like, 'what's wrong with you?' [...] Because I have my own child but I don't feel like that [...] When I'm with my friends who I know they like that kind of 'aww' thing, I wait for their reaction, and then after they reacted then I react the way they reacted.

While Mabedi's friends found many aspects of her self-described 'masculine' behaviour difficult to accept, Mabedi's ambivalence towards young children seemed to cause the most disturbance. With motherhood considered innate for women, failing to be overcome with emotion in the presence of babies may be interpreted as both biological and sociocultural deviance. Mabedi's peers responded by accusing her of being masculine. Mabedi was distressed by the aspersions cast on her womanhood and responded by concealing aspects of her nature.

Though Mabedi identified unequivocally as a woman, she longed to share men's dominant status in society and often found herself conflicted between the social need to behave as a 'good woman' and the competitive drive to 'emulate men'. Such dissonance manifested in several ways; for example, in the way she drove her car: 'My friends say I'm always trying to drive like a man [...] I don't wanna drive like a woman. Because people tell you, driving like a woman, there is something wrong with it, if there's somebody that's causing traffic [...] it's like, "that woman!" So then I drive fast and I get into trouble.' Indeed, it has been shown that masculinity is correlated with greater incidence of driving offences and violations (Deniz et al., 2021). For Mabedi there was no way for women to 'win' on the road; driving at a responsible speed suggested irksome timidity, driving irresponsibly fast saw women judged as masculine. Driving thus made her feel that fundamentally, 'there's something wrong with the way I am'. Mabedi felt trapped by cultural expectations to present qualities associated with femininity, a labour of identity construction that she described as thankless. She emulated male behaviour as well as that of her female friends, struggling to locate and preserve her own sense of self.

Mabedi's presentation of traits considered masculine also caused discord at home, where she lived with her mother, father, brother and her own child:

My mum is always telling me, you know, 'you need to start acting like a woman so a man can see you and marry you' [...] my mum was like, 'nobody is gonna marry you if you're like this'. She feels like I'm too independent. Yes, this is the other thing also, when you are too independent and when you don't take nonsense, they call it being a man. So my mum is like, 'you're gonna have to learn to compromise, you're gonna have to learn to be a woman.'

Mabedi's mother's emphasis on deference as key to marriageability supports the notion that wives are expected to be subservient to their husbands, and highlights the view that women must demonstrate subservience to attract a husband in the first place. Given that marriage is a prerequisite for achieving womanhood, being labelled as unmarriageable effectively renders a woman culturally invisible. Mabedi's mother's behaviour illustrates the ways the patriarchal bargain manifests between generations of women – both through the gendered domestic labour arrangements she imposed in the home, discussed above, and through her attempts to shape Mabedi's character to that of a 'good Motswana woman'.

Though Mabedi's independence was not valued by her mother, it might have been appreciated by my participants. The culturally informed attributes considered necessary for the successful presentation of womanhood were, for at least half of the women in my study, different from the characteristics that they personally admired in other women. Fifteen of my participants outwardly expressed that they valued traits such as independence and courage, which might be considered somewhat incompatible with the feminine communal attributes that exemplified customary standards of womanhood. My interviewees valued: 'a woman who knows what she wants, who is not afraid to voice out her opinion, no matter how different it is from other people' (Kesegofetse); who has a 'strong character' (Malisa); is 'independent' and 'stands up for themselves' (Tumelo); who is 'resilient' (Pono); who will 'get up and do [...] who is unshaken' (Beth); will 'stand up and fight for their rights' (Emelda); who have 'confidence [...] believing in themselves' (Khana); does not 'rely on men' (Thato) and 'has a dream, yeah. I want a woman who doesn't give in to the situation at hand. I want a woman who would stand up and fight' (Tsala). While these women valued traits such as resilience and self-reliance, they perceived that others would find such qualities distasteful in a woman. These participants emphasized the ability of women to fight, stand up for themselves and endure adversity, indicating the widespread expectation of hardship in the lives of women. Daymond et al. (2003: 506) show that historic Setswana initiation songs emphasize the 'merits of endurance and perseverance during hardships' for women; for example:

> I dig hard clay,
> Womanhood is a hardship,
> Yes, yes, womanhood is a hardship,
> Yes, yes, womanhood is a hardship,
> Please help me dig this clay,
> Womanhood is a hardship

Using distancing language such as 'they expect' or 'you are supposed to be' when talking about cultural expectations of conventional feminine qualities, it was apparent that my participants did not necessarily see traits such as subservience or humility as appealing in women on a personal level. Lesedi, for example, valued 'somebody who could be firm, regardless of being a woman', further illustrating the perceived incompatibility of women with assertiveness. While positioning womanhood and resolve as mutually exclusive, she appreciated determination in women that she knew, signifying a disconnect between traits she valued in a woman and traits she deemed womanly. Akhu and Thato considered that women were more resilient than men in the face of adversity because of the pressure on women to carry financial and care obligations for the family and wider community. However, they did not see such a view as culturally common. Research has shown a disconnect between how individuals think society expects women and men to behave (and how they think they do behave), and their personal beliefs about how women and men should behave (Ridgeway, 2011). For example, 'holding gender stereotypes as descriptive beliefs about how men and women usually are is only modestly correlated with ideological beliefs about gender egalitarianism' (Ridgeway, 2011: 62). My interviews suggest the existence of such a pattern among my participants, and speak to the mutable and complex nature of individual expectations and perceptions of gendered traits in women and men.

Basadi described her family as being full of 'strong independent women', both in her mother's generation and her own. In her experience, women 'have always had a very big role to play in villages, in households, in families'. She depicted Botswana as a 'matriarchal society', although she conceded that 'women defer to men culturally'. Thus, it appeared that while women were ultimately expected to be deferential to men, some were influential in their homes and communities. Certainly the notion that women in patriarchal societies may find limited authority in the domestic sphere has been examined (e.g., see Gilmore, 1990; Rogers, 1975; Shu et al., 2012). Though decision-making power in the home was not explored in detail for this study, the notion of female dominance in the household was not borne out through my interviews, in which the home was largely represented as a site of inequality, disappointment and even violence. Overall, the interviewees offered a complex view of women's character; the participants perceived that traditionally a woman was expected to be compassionate, humble and submissive, and some of the participants agreed these traits to be necessary in the 'proper' presentation of womanhood. However, many of the interviewees valued strong, self-determining women, and were in fact autonomous in thought and action themselves.

An important aspect of the enforcement of femininity is through the regulation of women's appearance and particularly their clothing, which is a conveniently visible signifier. An early US study notes that imposing clothing rules on men and women 'forces people to "wear" their gender for all to see, setting the stage for differential treatment' (Whisner, 1982: 76). In the context of patriarchy, clothing rules contribute to the 'perpetration and sanction of sexual objectification' of women, which reduces women to the reactions they provoke in men (Whisner, 1982: 77). Sexual objectification of women is legitimized and codified in law and policy, for example in the United States, through rules that prevent schoolgirls from wearing trousers so as not to 'distract' schoolboys, or in criminalizing public bare-breastedness for women (but not for men) to prevent men's sexual arousal and the ensuing public disruption (Whisner, 1982). The formal rules of democratic societies are culturally determined, reflecting and reinforcing the values and priorities of the dominant system or group. Where clothing regulations are formally or informally dictated by a patriarchal order, 'women in particular are often compelled to appear in certain ways that symbolize their subordinate position in society' (Whisner, 1982: 73).

When I asked my participants about what was expected of a 'good Motswana woman', more than half indicated that conservative clothing choices were considered a crucial element of feminine respectability: 'Culturally you are supposed to cover up. You're supposed to be humble, to have respect and to be diligent' (Tshepiso). For rural women of all ages, modesty in dress was closely tied to humility and obedience: 'I have to have respect, being a woman, behaving like a woman. Wearing like a woman. Not, in Botswana we don't prefer to be seen in a mini skirt as a woman. You are supposed to be wearing something that covers your knees. So that you can be recognised as a woman' (Khana). Revealing the legs and head were considered particularly inappropriate, with trousers and short skirts seen as improper by several of my participants: 'You will still find one or two with the mini skirts [...] trousers are not allowed and you should cover your head, and just dressing properly as a woman' (Malisa).

Though the specific types of clothing deemed appropriate for women vary by context, 'what is shared is the idea that *some* way of appearing makes a woman too sexual for the given context and that it is proper to control whether and when women appear that way' (Whisner, 1982: 108). Reneilwe described her acceptance of the social control of women's clothing as a legitimate form of gender regulation: 'What are they going to say when I walk outside with just mini skirts? [...] But that is a way of helping us grow, as responsible people.' She spoke of her personal embodied shame, perhaps indicating her internalization of women's sexual objectification: 'Deep down I knew, you see I have that shame as a woman, my body shouldn't be seen. Just imagine if I would say, "I don't care, I do what I like", no one is going to respect me. Honestly, no one.'

Though the urban participants largely agreed with prevailing views that women should dress conservatively, such expectations were met with resistance by some of the urban women I spoke to. Mpho shared an example of how her resistance manifested in her daily life:

> It was summer, and I was wearing a summer dress [...] And this man behind me [...] he was muttering about how inappropriately I was dressed. Which, it was funny to me because I was like, I don't think it's inappropriate and I don't think anybody that I know would have thought it was inappropriate [...] he was just like, shocked.

Mayer (1999: 17–18) posits that 'when men (and sometimes older women) control the "proper behaviour" of women, in effect they control women's bodies and sexuality'. Mpho's anecdote offers an explicit example of such control – the man appeared to think it was his right to police Mpho's clothing, and by extension, her body and expression of self. However, Mpho's inherent rejection of patriarchal social control was implied in her amusement that a man would judge her clothing in such a way; her light-hearted approach to the incident indicated that she did not consider his views worthy of concern.

Basadi, who had a similar education level and international experience to Mpho, and was also from the city, felt 'stifled' around 'very conservative people [...] who care too much about what other people think or what other people will say, what other people are wearing'. Both Mpho and Basadi gave the impression that their exposure to alternative lifestyles through higher education and travel minimized the impact of certain conservative norms on their lives, particularly in relation to rules around gendered clothing. However, many of my rural participants, who had fewer resources and limited exposure to society beyond their village, were deeply affected by others' perceptions of their physical presentation as women in the world.

Managing male dominance

For some of the women in my study, the careful navigation of male dominance was necessary for the successful performance of womanhood. Women manage patriarchal authority on a daily basis in their homes, workplaces, churches and communities, which translates to considerable physical, economic, mental and emotional labour. Such labour manifests in various visible and invisible forms, as I show below.

Tumelo lamented that women were obligated to serve their uncles and other men in the community, regardless of whether they felt such service was deserved: 'I really feel men are, I don't know, they are spoon-fed [...] we really give them a whole lot of respect, yet some of them they don't even deserve that respect.' She elaborated:

> And I don't know if this is because it's biblical, there is a lot of respect for men in my culture. Even when the man is useless, I can tell them he is useless, and all he does is go to the bar and come back, go to sleep, then go to the bar in the morning, come back and sleep. You will be respecting this uncle of yours, you know, you will be washing his laundry, cleaning up after

him [...] Men are treated with a lot of respect, they don't do much, they are favoured.

Tumelo considered that high regard for men stemmed from biblical notions of patriarchal authority. Since 79 per cent of the population identify as Christian (CIA, 2022), the biblical view of women as inferior to men is potentially influential. The impact of religious and spiritual beliefs about womanhood is outside of the scope of this study but is an important area for further enquiry. Like many of my participants Tumelo expressed a poor view of men, describing them as lazy, 'useless' and irresponsible, and as failed providers. Similarly, the Kenyan women in Silberschmidt's (2001: 661–2) study complained of men drinking heavily and failing to contribute positively to the lives of their families or partners. While these women 'generally recognized and accepted certain formal rights and privileges that were reserved for men, they had no illusions about men as conscientious providers'. The men in Silberschmidt's study admitted that they drank to escape the uncertainty presented by a changing socioeconomic environment. Since I did not interview Batswana men I cannot offer a male perspective, however, Mookodi's (2004) research indicates that like Kenyan men, Batswana men are struggling with comparable uncertainty as a result of socioeconomic shifts and changing gender relations, as discussed above. Certainly it is a common sight in Botswana to see taverns filled with men drinking alcohol during day and night, accompanied by few if any women.

The interviews indicated that men were the primary decision makers in the family. While women might be consulted about major decisions, 'whatever a man says, it's law and that's it [...] if he doesn't want to sell a car [...] renovate that house, you can't say anything [...] that is that' (Keatlaretse); men have 'always been the ones who decide for the family. Who decide for women' (Mpho). Women's lack of authority in decision making was further illustrated by the likening of wives to children: 'Men are head of the house, and sometimes the women can be referred to as the children to the husband' (Pono). Men's authority in decision making extended beyond finance and household matters; they exercised control over women's bodies, too.

Though unprompted by my interview questions, some of the participants chose to share that men usually decide the number and timing of children born: 'Sometimes [women] do not always have the final say in defining how many children they should have' (Kesegofetse). Thato agreed, 'the man will be wanting whatever he wants, and for sure you are going to become pregnant'. Emelda shared that men in her life had demanded she have more children. One said to her: '"I want two kids, I want a boy, these are girls only, I want a boy." So he is deciding for you.' Thato, Kesegofetse and Emelda's assertions suggest that some women have marginal control over the size of their families, despite their major role in raising and providing for their children. Lenah ascribed men's reproductive decision-making power to the practice of *lobola*: 'After paying that, the men kind of own you.' The cultural perception of men as the dominant decision makers limits women's ability to self-determine in many aspects of their lives, including in the reproductive sphere.

Cultural reverence for men is demonstrated through gendered interactions at public gatherings. The construction of womanhood as a subservient position is displayed through the practice of food service, in which 'women have to give [men] food, women have to eat last, after feeding the men' (Reneilwe). Women's inferior status is underscored by seating arrangements at such events, where 'a man can't stand up while a woman is sitting down. She has to stand [...] they sit on the chair, then the women sit on the floor or lie on the mat' (Reneilwe). The appearance of male dominance, its visual display, appears to be at least equally important as its reality. Keatlaretse described a typical village scene which illuminates how male dominance is displayed even in instances where it is physically impractical: 'You see a woman struggling to carry a child on her back and a bag on her head, and then the husband is just carrying a jacket [...] You ask her, "why are you doing that? Why can't the man carry the bag instead? Or the kid?" And they say, "no, you don't say that to a man".' Keatlaretse explained that for the man to share in the physical burden of carrying children and luggage would be to suggest that he is assisting with domestic labour, with 'women's work'. Though he might carry out such tasks in private, he risks challenge to his masculinity should he do so in public.

While some of my participants were accepting of male dominance, and others were simply resigned to it, ten of the women I spoke to openly resented the implications of an inequitable gender order. Some women actively fought against it while others resisted more subtly, typically through behavioural or lifestyle choices. In this manner a minority of my interviewees were able to maintain lifestyles that were relatively autonomous while upholding the appearance of patriarchal power at a level deemed acceptable in Tswana culture, thus preserving their standing as women in the community.

Shera, whose concerns about unequal domestic labour distribution between her and her partner were discussed above, was also dealing with gendered expectations of her behaviour in other areas of her life. For example, her purchase of a truck caused discord within the community: "'You're driving a truck?! What are you doing with a truck?!' [...] And my aunt was like, "yes, you should really get a man who has a truck" [...] whatever, I bought the truck.' With trucks perceived as powerful, masculine vehicles they are considered unsuitable for women to drive and own, and Shera's community was shocked by her purchase. Her aunt's proposal that Shera date a man who owned a truck as an alternative is indicative of gendered policing as a form of social control among senior women, and evidences the patriarchal bargain in action (Kandiyoti, 1988). The male truck seller also attempted to preserve gendered norms around vehicle ownership, even though his success in doing so would have cost him a sale. Shera recalled their exchange: "Ah, you know my sister, I need to give you advice [...] do you have a man?" and I said yes, he's like, "well, I don't know if you should be buying all these trucks, because you know, how is he handling it? You know, you really don't want to make them feel inferior." Ultimately Shera purchased the truck and accepted the social fallout.

In another example, she chose to manipulate a situation to preserve the appearance of her partner's superiority and avoid negative social judgement of her actions. Shera owned a plot of land and was planning to commission the building of a house on the plot, an independent decision that did not involve her partner. This choice caused concern among her family and friends, who told Shera: "'You need to involve him' [...] 'Where is your man in this?'" Initiating a construction project single-handedly was socially problematic, achieving home ownership before her partner had achieved the same was even more so:

> I knew he needed to get a house because if I finish my house before he had a house, it would be an issue. Not necessarily for him, okay maybe it would become an issue for him, but definitely his friends, his community, whatever, would think this was an issue [...] I'm looking for houses for him because I need this man to have a house. [...] But we all know behind the scenes we are negotiating some very serious ego-stroking bullshit.

For Shera to own a home while her partner continued to rent property would imply that she was more independent or successful than him, undermining his masculinity and culturally mandated superiority. Shera felt compelled to invest additional resources to address the imbalance. Such a tactic was effective in appeasing her friends, family and her partner while allowing her to pursue her ambitions, yet it demanded emotional labour and took up extra time in a busy schedule. Shera expressed disbelief in discovering she was required to handle expectations in such a way, but conceded, 'apparently it matters [...] now I have to manage these things'.

While all of my participants accepted some level of male dominance, many asserted personal boundaries in protecting individual values that were misaligned with cultural norms. Lesedi broke ties with a boyfriend 'because his word was final'. She had felt strongly for this man and hoped they would build a lasting connection, but ultimately she could not live with his domineering character and assumption of control within their relationship. Lesedi also challenged male authority in matters of inheritance. One of five siblings, she fought openly against a family decision that favoured her single male sibling over the four sisters: 'They said [...] "the four of you, you have to share this 25 hectares, and [he] is having 25 hectares".' Lesedi's family argument had continued for years, and since her sisters did not wish to challenge their brother she lacked their support in the conflict. Nonetheless, she was determined not to concede until she was allocated a share of land equal to that of her brother. Though her continued battle was a drain on her mental and physical resources, she considered it a matter of principle that the siblings inherit equal proportions of land and refused to accept her brother's decision on the matter. As was the case for Shera, refusing to be passive in the face of male authority demanded considerable time and investment of resources. Given that women already carry extensive burdens of responsibility in most areas of their lives, the additional work of resisting culturally informed gender arrangements was unwelcome. Nonetheless, for these participants it was an inevitable cost, necessary for preserving their autonomy in the areas where it mattered to them most.

Connell (2011: 74) has shown that social convention is not disembodied. Rather, it operates through human behaviour to delineate 'possibilities for action'. Though patriarchal authority carries advantages for men, in some cases they may be financially or socially disadvantaged by gendered expectations that limit their possibilities for action. As discussed above, Lenah's husband helped her with domestic tasks only in private for fear of the social repercussions of being seen to invert gendered norms. A comparable dynamic limited Lenah and her husband's choice of settlement. She explained: 'I come from Kgalagadi, my husband comes from Serowe. So we can't say we are settling in Kgalagadi, you know. We can't settle in Kgalagadi [...] We can't, everybody would be laughing at us, even if there were opportunities in Kgalagadi [...] He says, "ah, people are going to laugh at me! They will say I'm the one married".'

Lenah and her husband wanted to make use of a financial opportunity to build a house in her home region, but they were prevented from doing so by the gendered custom of women moving away from their homes and into their husband's settlement upon marriage. At the time of the interview they lived in the capital city, but since neither party was born there it was considered neutral ground in relation to gendered rules about settlement. Should they relocate to either of their home villages customary determinants of location would be activated, along with their accompanying restrictions. For a couple to build property in the wife's village would undermine the husband's standing and subject him to ridicule. The final line of the above quotation highlights an important view of marriage as a gendered process – the man marries the woman, he is the active subject. When a couple's choices invert gender norms they are accused of role switching – she becomes the active subject, and his masculinity is undermined.

Tshiamo and her partner experienced similar judgement of the gendered dynamics of their union. Since her partner was unemployed, Tshiamo had established a small store for them to run together so they could both generate income to support the family. She hoped that if she was able to organize a source of paid work for her partner, he would be finally accepted by her mother as a suitable provider after years of unemployment. However, this plan did not have the effect Tshiamo anticipated; the initiative she showed in starting the business suggested a level of autonomy that was seen to undermine her partner's dominance as the man of the house. In taking strategic action to ensure a dual income, she attracted social judgement of the power balance in their home:

In my case, my partner is willing us to get married, and my mother is complaining and saying that I'm the one who is going to pay *lobola*. Eh. He is operating the tuck shop. We are saving money. And my mother is not taking that as his money. She says this tuck shop, for it to be established it was my initiative. [...] My mum says when we get married it will be me paying *lobola*, because he is not a man. Because I make the money, it means I am the man. He works in the tuck shop but it is my idea. [...] When he pays *lobola* my mum says I will be the one paying *lobola* for myself.

The costs of womanhood: An overview

The cost of womanhood is high. Women of all ages, settlement categories, levels of education and types of employment are subject to unyielding claims on their time and other resources in the public and private spheres, whether they are married or single, with children or without. Faced with demanding obligations to their extended families and wider community in addition to attending to the needs of their husbands and children, women are often so encumbered that they experience most aspects of their lives as labour. Their labour supports the structures of patriarchy, freeing men to pursue careers or independent projects and to participate in leisure activities, while limiting women's opportunities for personal fulfilment and economic advancement. Certain irreconcilabilities stem from the requirement of women to meet culturally sanctioned standards of femininity, while doing what is necessary to maintain a level of autonomy and survive materially in a rapidly changing socioeconomic environment. While the gender myth of the fragile, submissive woman is pervasive, women's lived experience necessitates resilience and resourcefulness. The costs of womanhood that my interviewees described were typically informed by customary expectations of women to perform a litany of tasks under the weight of patriarchal authority. However, the participants who rejected, resisted or modified gendered traditions were likely to incur additional costs in the form of social challenge and expectation management. In the following chapter I investigate the interplay of traditional mores with the forces of modernization and globalization, and women's diversity of experience in the effects of cultural transition.

Notes

1   The terms *bogadi* and *lobola* may be used interchangeably to refer to bride price. I use *lobola* throughout this book since that is the term I heard used most commonly during my time in Botswana, but some of the citations I use in this thesis refer to bride price as *bogadi*.

2   While the distribution of occupation types in my sample is well aligned with national distribution, any representativeness is coincidental, and is likely attributable to the sampling biases inherent in the personal network and snowballing methods I used to recruit participants. I share the distribution of occupation types, and elsewhere of other characteristics among my sample, for context only.

3   A term referring to the widely acknowledged (unofficial) limit on the advancement of marginalized groups into senior positions in the workplace, particularly women.

4   I would be remiss not to note that men, too, participate in kin support systems. For example, I recall a personal instance where a male Motswana friend and his brothers each contributed cash towards the repair of a family member's broken washing machine. However, examples of kin provision that my interviewees shared related to other women and this has shaped my focus here.

5

'The life of women has changed very, very much': Womanhood in transition?

–Thato

Gender inequality has proven resilient to major social and economic changes worldwide. For example, as Ridgeway (2011: 3) has shown in the contemporary United States, 'a gender hierarchy that advantages men over women survived the profound social and economic reorganization that accompanied the transition of the United Stated from an agrarian to an industrialized society.' Ridgeway (2011) attributes the persistence of gender inequality in the United States to the continued use of sex and gender to categorize and define social relations. As such, patriarchal codes are re-established and preserved in emerging social and economic configurations. In Hong Kong and the United Kingdom too, Jackson et al. (2013) have demonstrated that gendered inequalities continue to affect women despite the increased opportunities brought by global economic and social shifts. For example, women remain primarily responsible for caring for children and their career options are limited by cultural segregation (Jackson et al., 2013). Ridgeway (2011: 159) notes that the 'central, underlying factor that allows inequality to persist is the way that changes in cultural beliefs about gender lag changes in material arrangements based on gender.' Certainly this analysis resonates with the accounts given by the women I interviewed, who endure gendered disadvantages in the face of potentially field-levelling social and economic transitions.

As previous chapters have shown, Botswana has experienced remarkable changes in its sociocultural, economic and political environment since it achieved independence from the United Kingdom in 1966. It has seen the impact of several key forces of modernity, including capitalism, globalization, technological advance, urbanization and individualism. Such forces impact women to varying degrees, and their effects were articulated in different ways by my participants depending on their generation, class, settlement type and other background variables. It is not the purpose of this chapter to document the nature and extent of every shift affecting Batswana women. Rather, I examine the transitions that seemed to be meaningful to my participants, that is, those they raised in response to open questions about changes that they have personally observed and experienced. My participants' diverse interpretations of these shifts help to shape an analysis of the gendered impact of a society in transition. Throughout this book I have referred to tensions that can arise when the processes and values of the past clash with those of the present. In this chapter I look more closely at these dynamics, investigating the extent to which competing cultural norms might co-exist or even merge, 'modified and reshaped in new historical circumstances, whether through deliberate revival or simply adaptations of everyday mores and practices' (Jackson et al., 2013: 669).

My interviewees often posited 'tradition' as the antithesis of modernity, conceptualizing tradition as a fixed set of practices, values and behaviours rooted firmly in an unchanging past, which is itself constructed as a static and indisputable reality. Scholars have argued for a view of tradition that recognizes it as adaptive, its practices not precluded by modern social and economic conditions, and for a view of the past that acknowledges its continued construction and reconstruction through narrative (Jackson et al., 2013; Hobsbawm and Ranger, 1983/2015; Hunter, 2009; Phillips, 2004). Hobsbawm and Ranger (1983/2015) posit that traditions are often invented during periods of rapid social transformation, for example, during the colonial era. In the African case, colonial and local leaders and anthropologists collaborated in 'colonial codification' of custom, forging a sense of permanence that distorts the pre-colonial reality of flexible and constructive cultural practices. Further, the official record of customary laws, systems, beliefs and so on was informed by and taken down by men; male dominance was 'expressed even more clearly in colonial invented custom than it had ever been before' (Ranger, 1983/2015: 258). Thus, when I consider my participants' engagement with tradition and Botswana's cultural past, I am not seeking to trace or challenge the history and origin of the customs they described as traditional.[1] Rather, I attempt to honour their interpretations while remaining mindful of the constructed and or invented nature of tradition, particularly in the African colonial context.

Gender relations and women's autonomy

Twenty of my participants stated that young women today have more independence than their grandmothers; perceiving that while women conventionally 'relied mostly on men, now they get up and do stuff for themselves' (Beth). Whether avoiding dependence on men stems from choice or necessity, the fact that self-reliance is an option at least demonstrates the possibility of autonomy for women. The dominance of this narrative among my sample not only supports its legitimacy but demonstrates a level of collective consciousness, a shared story of women's growing empowerment that was borne out in the lives of my participants in different ways. Speaking of men's dominance over women Malisa observed, 'it is not as bad as it used to be in the past [but] one way or the other, they will still see that you are a woman. [...] Things are better than before.' Malisa noted an improvement in women's status that was nonetheless tempered by the resilient perception of women as innately inferior. Still, she hoped for continued progress towards gender equity and at forty-three, believed it was within the realm of possibility for future generations, if not for her.

The majority of my participants were aware of the disadvantages women faced in the context of a patriarchal order, and of the changes Botswana had begun to see in this respect. Ngoma Leslie (2006) attributes the spread of political consciousness to the women's movement in Botswana, arguing that the movement's rights discourse reached and influenced ordinary homes and families. Those among my sample with high levels of education were more likely to speak of changes in gender relations within a rights framework; however, rights-based narratives were not exclusive to educated participants. Beth's education ended halfway through secondary school, yet she was conscious of the political context of changes in gender relations: 'Nowadays people know their rights, so women are no longer, their rights are no longer violated like before, they stand for themselves and speak out.' Ona had similar educational attainment, yet she was confident in articulating that women were 'not just the shadows of men anymore. In politics, in work, they have their own say'. Thus, while political consciousness was strongest among the most educated of my sample, its influence was perceptible across the board.

Mabedi pointed to increasing political consciousness as a factor in women gaining autonomy:

> Researcher: How are things different for you than they were for your mother's and grandmothers' generations?
>
> Mabedi: [...] We are still fighting to be equal to men. I think for my grandmother, during their time, they weren't even bothered. Like they didn't realise there was the need to be. It was like, 'why do you wanna be equal to a man? Let him be a man'. Yeah, so I think um, that's what's different between me and my grandmother. And I think the transition period was during my mum's time.

Mabedi's story suggests a changing state of consciousness during her mother's generation, the beginnings of an important shift away from essentialist notions of gender. Importantly, Mabedi noted a 'transition period', during which a change in attitudes towards gender equality took place. Her phrasing implies a hermetically sealed moment, a movement for change that had since ceased. Similarly, Keeya considered that for her grandmother, being a homemaker was 'not by choice [...] it was the right thing to do. You took care of your family, your home, for everybody, all the time'. Her mother, however, 'went to school, she studied, she's always worked', and so Keeya could 'see a big difference between maybe my mum and her mum, myself and my grandmother, but between me and my mother, not so much'. Several other participants perceived important shifts in women's empowerment between their grandmothers' and mothers' generations, but comparative stagnation in gender politics since then. My interviewees' perspectives are supported by Bauer's (2011) observation that the women's movement peaked in the 1980s and 1990s, tapering off once it had met its primary goals of legislative reform and the initiation of women into parliament. Bauer recognizes several factors contributing to the decline of the movement, including overwhelming social problems such as rural poverty and the HIV/AIDS epidemic, an uninterested head of state, a constitution that is not explicitly egalitarian, public apathy, lost external funding as a result of Botswana achieving middle-income status, internal divisions and weak organization, and movement leaders entering government positions (Bauer, 2011).

Though my participants overwhelmingly pointed to the home as the locus of gender inequality, a minority observed that the grip of patriarchy in the domestic sphere might be loosening. Emelda spoke of the decline of men's decision-making power within the home: 'As you grow up, you knew that the man was the head of the family. He is the one that takes decisions. But right now, things are coming good.' Neo, who was thirty and from the city, recalled that when she was younger her father expected women or girls in the household to bring him water in a bowl and assist in washing his hands before meals. Now, however, her father would 'go to the bathroom, wash his [own] hands'. Neo explained that expectations of women as the 'servants of men' were 'a bit firmer' when she was younger. In another example, she recounted stories of women sitting on the floor at public events so that men could sit in chairs (a practice mentioned in the previous chapter), a time-honoured norm that had 'gone down' as people had 'become a bit more open-minded over time'. Since the household is typically the last site of social change, the decline of symbolic markers of male dominance in the domestic environment is significant, albeit in the context of continued and widespread subjugation of women in the home as shown in earlier chapters of this book.

Nonetheless, Neo qualified her comments with the suggestion that changing gender relations in the home are limited to urban areas. In rural settlements, inequality is 'still pretty much the same as it was a long time ago' (Neo). Her view was shared by women from both urban and rural locations. Twenty-nine of my participants spoke of an urban-rural divide in women's role and status,[2] indicating a widespread awareness of difference that was supported in the personal accounts of many of the women I spoke to. Kesegofetse, a highly educated rural woman, shared that in villages like hers, 'culturally it's okay for women to be victims of men', whereas 'city women are empowered, they don't take a lot of rubbish from men'. She reasoned that since urban women were more likely to be financially independent because of greater opportunities for education and employment, they could choose to live outside of gendered constraints. By and large this was not indicated in my interviews. As I have argued elsewhere, the women I spoke to who were self-sufficient, whether rural or urban, struggled with gendered constraints on their autonomy to some extent. Keatlaretse, who lived in the city, claimed that in villages, 'whatever a man says, it's law and that's it'. Reneilwe, a rural woman who worked in the city, agreed and gave examples of the expression of male dominance, including the practice of physical separation at public events such as weddings and funerals: 'You can't see [women and men] in one place; traditionally they will say, man has to sit that side.' Reneilwe 'could not imagine surviving that life' but suggested that 'maybe if I was at the village I [would] have no choice', illustrating the perceived influence of gendered barriers in rural areas by those living in urban locations. Although Reneilwe expressed disdain for certain cultural practices that positioned women as inferior to men she embraced others, and rejected gender equality on the whole, as discussed earlier. The apparent thread of contradiction running through Reneilwe's opinions and life choices is suggestive of the agency some women might employ in their selective acceptance of cultural norms. She was able to choose a career in the male-dominated STEM industry, while at the same time articulating a strong preference for the gendered division of labour in the home and seeking to become a servile wife. The level of agency shown by Reneilwe in rejecting some expressions of male dominance and accepting others was not typical of rural participants.

Tensions between gendered expectations of the performance of womanhood between rural and urban settlements affected several of my participants, particularly those whose lives were distributed between multiple sites. Tumelo lived in Mochudi, a village outside of the capital Gaborone. She worked in Gaborone as an auditor. Her extended family remain in her home village of Serowe. She spoke of the restrictions she encounters whenever she returns to Serowe:

> Tumelo: Our culture has really changed, yeah. But where I come from
>   they still expect me to be that woman. [...] They expect me to do those
>   duties that a woman does. [...] A well-behaved woman, I guess.
> Researcher: Are expectations different when you're [in the city] to when
>   you're in Serowe?
> Tumelo: Eish! They are, they are very different. They are very different. [...]
>   Obviously when I'm at home, with the old women, I have to be living
>   a certain way, you see. Because that's kind of expected of me. But when
>   I'm here in the city, I do things my way. When I'm here I'm on my own
>   so I get to do what I want.

Tumelo elaborated that women's position within Tswana culture had improved in many ways, and she felt she could act independently most of the time. Yet, when she returned to her village her freedom was limited by conservative expectations of how a woman should behave; financial self-sufficiency did not exempt her from the restrictive cultural practices that persist in rural areas. Her reference to 'the old women' suggests that her female elders had as much, if not more of a role to play in maintaining and reproducing the patriarchal system than men themselves. Tsala, a postgraduate who was in a financially stable dual-income marriage, also spoke of the limitations her mother and the wider community imposed on her when she returned to her home village: 'When I am back at home, I don't only belong to my mother, I belong to the society.' However, Tsala found a level of independence away from the surveillance of her family. When living in the city she found: 'I can live better than that. I can be something different than what I am [back home].' Mothers, aunts, sisters and grandmothers criticized and discouraged young women's expressions of autonomy away from home, further evidencing the phenomenon of cultural collusion in support of the patriarchal bargain (Kandiyoti, 1988).

The interviews suggested that mothers and grandmothers, having gained a level of status through childbearing and age, tended to hold more social influence than their daughters and granddaughters. Yet, younger women perceived that older women's subservience to men was intensified and preserved by the grip of patriarchal norms on older generations. Pamela observed that even in the capital where many young women were enjoying weakening gender restrictions, 'there are still some women who can't get [out] from under men, especially older women. Because this independence thing is the new generation.' Thus, while the rural/urban divide impacted the level of autonomy women held, generational differences were also evident, supporting Bourn's (2008) assertion that social change tends to leave older people behind.

Education, employment and political participation

Many of my participants perceived beneficial changes in girls' education over recent generations and were confident that girls were encouraged to value education and enabled to achieve it: 'To get educated over and above, that would be normal' (Neo), 'you can study as much as you want, get the highest levels of education' (Pono). Lesedi, who was a teacher, claimed: 'We are so fortunate [...] most of our grandmothers are not educated [...] a boy child was given that opportunity to go to school, and then the girl child was left behind. [...] But now we could see some changes.' Contrary to Lesedi's assertion, during her grandmother's generation schooling for all children was 'zealously' encouraged by tribal chiefs and foreign missionaries, and many more girls than boys were able to attend since boys were needed at the cattle posts (Schapera, 1940). A 1977 government review of the education system recommended 'Universal Education for All' as a national principle (Makwinja-Morara, 2009). The ratio of girls-to-boys enrolling in school has hovered close to equal for decades and has frequently been higher for girls (World Bank, 2022). For example, in the village of Mochudi, 83 per cent of the children attending school in 1937 were girls (Schapera, 1940).

Nonetheless, Lesedi's perception of girls as having less access to education in the past perhaps stems from the notion that education is more beneficial to boys than girls, as girls' education is taken less seriously (Makwinja-Morara, 2009: 442). Additionally, girls face barriers to their schooling after enrolment – they are quick to be kept home should their domestic services be required and drop-out rates for pregnant girls have long been considered a 'serious national problem' (Makwinja-Morara, 2009). Emelda, who was forty-two and grew up in a village, reflected on the barriers she had faced to her childhood education: 'We were living in a village, it's not like in town. And our mothers were old women who doesn't care if you go to school or don't go to school. If you don't go to school you will be home making domestic jobs, and they are fine with that. [...] She will say, "You are not going to school today, you will look after your brothers and sisters at home".' The prioritization of girls' household labour over their schooling is ubiquitous in low-income nations worldwide, where 'education means a trade-off, usually between obtaining food and going to school' for those living in poverty (Stromquist, 2001: 43).

Educational attainment has an important effect on earning capacity; 67 per cent of those with tertiary education were employed in 2009/10 compared with 48 per cent of those with primary or lower education (World Bank, 2015). Lesedi reflected on the link between education and economic autonomy: 'We are now being educated, yeah it changed our life because it empower us. [...] The girl child was just being put back home, as somebody will marry her and take care of [her]. But now, now we can see we are empowered. Even me, I could be a breadwinner to my family.' New employment opportunities made it increasingly possible for women to support themselves and their families financially. Thato, who was thirty, remarked on the significance of formal employment for her generation: 'I find I am financially free, I can take care of my kid, I can do whatever I want with my money. Which was not the case with my mother.' For Tshiamo, being able to fund 'school fees, buy food for children, buy clothes' herself was the life-changing result of increased economic opportunity for women.

As Malisa explained, uneducated women 'spend most of their time in the field, some would be housewives, taking care of the kids [...] Most women work [for wages] now, not like before'. Women's entrance into the market economy was considered an important change by many of my participants, who raised it in response to my open question, 'what has changed for women?' Kesegofetse was enthusiastic about the possibility of leadership positions for women in the workplace: 'Some of them have even taken senior positions', a move she said was 'quite a positive change', and Neo asserted that women 'are expected in some parts of society to be ambitious [...] to achieve'. Likewise, Akhu reflected that women are now 'CEOs and directors of companies and even starting their own business', as she was in the process of doing herself. Keeya perceived that many industries had newly opened up for women over her lifetime; when she was young, 'women would be nurses and teachers' only, but 'in that regard a lot has changed'. Akhu shared that 'people get thrilled' when she performed on the saxophone, 'playing instruments that are like, labelled for men, you know'. Tumelo suggested that although men and women did not have equal opportunities in the workplace, there had been enough 'progress in that area' to give women 'that little bit of independence'.

Notably, all seven of the participants who attributed women's gains to opportunities in education had degree-level education themselves, and most were urban. By contrast, most rural women saw little or no change in women's ability to improve their position through education or employment. Urbanization has restricted most formal employment options to cities and towns. As Maatla lamented, 'there's nothing; you can't even see an office anywhere' in the villages. While some women migrate to urban sites for work, the low quality of education in villages means many cannot gain the qualifications needed to find employment.

In 1986 six educated professional Batswana women set up Emang Basadi, a nongovernmental organization (NGO) whose initial focus was the reform of gender-discriminatory laws. Emang Basadi translates as 'stand up, women' in Setswana. This name was chosen in reference to the national anthem, which encourages women to 'stand up beside your men' while men 'stand up and defend the nation' (Van Allen, 2001: 43). Viewed by women and men as troublemakers influenced by countries in the Global North, 'the women's challenge was seen as an unwelcome attack on the peace and stability of the country' (Ngoma Leslie, 2006: 58). Emang Basadi's lobbyists were to find that references to 'inequality' and 'discrimination' had little purchase with local women, who did not understand or accept that discriminatory legislation affected them personally (Ngoma Leslie, 2006).

In response to the difficulties of getting women involved in politics, Emang Basadi set up the *Political Education Project*, which held educational workshops for the public. They taught women why their vote mattered and why it was important that they voted for candidates who represented them. The NGO also offered training and support to potential women candidates. As a result of Emang Basadi's work, the president nominated two women to parliament after the 1994 elections, and a further two were elected by the public. In 1999, two women were nominated and six elected, bringing the total proportion of women members of parliament (MPs) to 18 per cent, up from 5 per cent prior to the NGO's activism (Ngoma Leslie, 2006). The efforts of Emang Basadi helped to counter women's historical exclusion from politics. In the past, 'women took no part in the government of the tribe; they did not attend the tribal assemblies, and all the political offices were kept exclusively in the hands of men' (Schapera, 1940: 302).

Many of the women I spoke to were politically engaged and conscious of the significance of female leadership in government. For several of my participants who were over thirty-five, women's entry into the political sphere was the most significant change since their mothers' or grandmothers' generations. Tsala was optimistic that 'we have broken the ground' despite the small numbers of women in parliament. Women's entry into positions of power in government brought hope for other positive changes for women.

Campbell and Wolbrecht (2006: 244) note that 'female role models change the political socialization of young girls' in the United States, making girls more likely to take an interest in politics and to embark on political careers. Women's political participation was also seen as advancing women's progress in the south-eastern Botswana context, where women MPs were expected to 'empower other women' (Emelda) through legislation.

Only participants over the age of thirty-five spoke of women's participation in government as a meaningful shift for women. Such optimism was absent in my younger participants, who had not experienced the momentous first entry of women into government. In their lifetimes the promise of women decision-makers at the top had faltered. The women's movement was at its height in Botswana in the 1980s and 1990s (Bauer, 2011), but as it began to weaken the proportion of women MPs fell from 17 per cent in 2000 to 8 per cent in 2009 (World Bank, 2022). By 2019 this had risen again to 11 per cent, as noted in the introductory chapter, and has remained there since. Thus, despite Botswana's strong democratic record, it has failed to sustain significant numbers of women in parliament following the initial peak in 1999, and Ngoma Leslie (2006: 5) maintains, 'while modern Botswana has, in theory, embraced a democratic political climate and universalistic bureaucracy, in practice traditional patriarchal Tswana cultural values have prevailed'.

However, women's engagement in high-level politics is not restricted to central government and its local branches; it has become possible for a woman to be village chief or *dikgosi*, ruling through the *kgotla* assembly. Despite some local resistance, elders in Ramotswa selected Botswana's first female paramount chief, Mosadi Seboko, in 2001.[3] She was also appointed chairwoman of the House of Chiefs, which advises the government on customary matters (BBC News, 2003). The nineteenth-century *kgotla* system has continued to function in rural areas to the present day, working alongside the state government to administer the rural population. The political significance of the *kgotla* is shown in data that consistently put Botswana in the top two or three of eighteen African countries in terms of responsibility for conflict resolution and the perceived influence of and trust in traditional leaders by comparison to local government officials (Bauer, 2016).

Thus, women's ability to become *dikgosi* is potentially significant in two key ways. First, through their ability to represent women's interests at the decision-making level. Since domestic disputes are typically administered by customary, rather than common law courts (Patel, 2013), women chiefs have the authority to make decisions affecting the stronghold of gender relations – the familial home and community. They might also advance women's status through legislative reforms, either directly or by influencing other decision makers (Bauer, 2016). Bauer's (2016: 232) interviews with women chiefs indeed suggested that 'they would be more likely to confront women's "suffering" than their male colleagues.' Second, the existence of women chiefs, though low in number at just 'a few dozen' of the 2430 known chiefs, has an important symbolic representation effect, 'potentially altering gendered ideas about the roles of women and men in politics, raising awareness of what women can achieve as political actors and legitimizing them as political actors, or encouraging women to become involved themselves in politics as voters, activists, candidates, leaders' (Bauer, 2016: 224). Lesedi's observations demonstrate the symbolic representation effect of women chiefs: 'a girl child would not be a *dikgosi*, but now we can see that change'. For Lesedi, even a slight proportion of women chiefs was a meaningful marker of progress in women's empowerment and a source of personal optimism in her life.

Single motherhood and paternal absenteeism

Twenty-one of my participants conceptualized the high prevalence of single motherhood, as discussed in previous chapters, as a relatively new phenomenon. Though reliable historic data are hard to come by, data from recent years show an increase in the proportion of children born to single mothers from 76 per cent in 2011 (Statistics Botswana, 2014) to 84 per cent in 2019 (Statistics Botswana, 2021). Single motherhood has been shown to be associated with negative health and wellbeing outcomes on mothers and their children across sub-Saharan Africa and worldwide (Christopher et al., 2002; Clark and Hamplová, 2013; Creighton et al., 2009; Ntoimo and Odimegwu, 2014; Raymo, 2016). Seventeen of the women I interviewed were unmarried mothers and many were raised by single mothers themselves. Of those seventeen, at least nine received no financial support from the father(s) of their child(ren), who had no contact with their children at all. Three did receive some form of support, and the remaining five did not offer information about their child(ren)'s father(s). Of the twenty-two participants who talked about their own fathers, fourteen had some form of relationship with their father and eight had no relationship with their father.

My interviewees uniformly attributed the high prevalence of single motherhood to absenteeism among fathers, a trend that is supported in the data. Research concerning fatherhood in Botswana collectively indicates that fathers are 'at best, distant and, at worst, absent and irresponsible' (Datta, 2011: 124). Datta (2011) observed that paternal presence in children's lives has been considered optional for generations, with many of the men in her study reporting that their own fathers were as neglectful towards them as they are towards their own children. Paternal absenteeism is culturally sanctioned. A male participant in Datta's (2011: 1340) research stated, 'no shame is attached to fathers who are not looking after their children'. Lesedi's comments suggested a similar view: 'If you have fathered a child here in Botswana it is not a must that you should be taking care of them.' The father of Lesedi's child had visited just once in two years. Emelda concurred, 'in our culture most of the men don't want the kid, and if he doesn't want the kid then he will leave you alone'. Supporting Emelda's assertion, one of Datta's (2011: 130) male participants admitted that he would 'run away' if he impregnated a woman and did not want the child. Similarly, the East African participants in Silberschmidt's (2001) research complained that men engaged in irresponsible sexual behaviour and failed to provide for their families. In South Africa too, women have become 'indignant at men's unreliability' (Hunter, 2009: 136).

Out of concern for losing all contact with her child's father and, thus, losing the ability to claim child maintenance payments, Keatlaretse hoped to take advantage of the Affiliation Proceedings (Amendment) Act of 1999, legislation that provided for official documentation of paternity. The Act was designed to legitimize mothers' bids for child maintenance. However, in Keatlaretse's case the father was not present at the birth and she struggled to get him to sign the necessary papers acknowledging that he was the child's father. Putting the onus on women to prove the paternity of their children undermines the Act's effectiveness as a tool of support for single mothers (Datta, 2011). Several other participants mentioned the same limitations of the child maintenance system that Datta observes, including difficulties in tracking fathers down, inadequate rulings on payment amounts and having to travel to the courts monthly to collect payments that might or might not have materialized. As such, these interviewees considered that 'to rely on men is the last option' (Beth). Indeed, Letamo and Rakgoasi (2000) discovered that only 35 per cent of a sample of 2564 single mothers received any form of child support from their children's fathers.

The young women I spoke to acknowledged that men's irresponsible sexual conduct and failure to provide for their offspring was culturally acceptable, yet they resented men's unreliability and the gendered double standards of behaviour that informed such norms, indicating a changing level of consciousness in younger generations. Malisa attributed the lack of support she received from her child's father to him being 'irresponsible, having multiple partners and having too many children'. Researchers note that for Batswana men, frequent casual sex with multiple women is an important marker of masculinity (Datta, 2011; Ho-Foster et al., 2010). Similarly in Kenya, the challenges to male dominance wrought by socioeconomic change are met by men seeking frequent casual sexual encounters as a means to restoring a damaged sense of masculinity, making them 'feel like a man' (Silberschmidt, 2001: 662). High frequency of casual sexual encounters is not new; Schapera (1940: 243) observed promiscuity in young men, who 'prefer to swagger through the village streets and spend their time with the girls [...] whom they are then able to seduce fairly easily'.

Multiple studies of sexual behaviour in Botswana have observed that condom use is inconsistent, despite widespread knowledge that condoms prevent pregnancy and HIV infection, and the fact that condoms are free and widely available (Kanda and Mash, 2018; Keetile and Letamo, 2015; Marandu and Chamme, 2004). Marandu and Chamme (2004) observe that men are more likely to align themselves with beliefs that discourage condom use. Women in societies with gender inequality at the society and community level have less ability to insist on contraceptive use, particularly those who are socioeconomically disadvantaged, undereducated, rural, victims of gender-based violence or financially dependent on their sexual partner (Closson et al., 2018; Jordan Smith, 2009; Weiser et al., 2007). As such, condom rejection behaviours in men are associated with major health risks for women. Closson et al. (2018: 3–4) assert that 'women's health and agency in the ability to negotiate HIV-prevention behaviours in sexual relationships is influenced by hegemonic norms of masculinity and unequal power in sexual relationships', thus, women suffer reduced agency in negotiating male condom use worldwide. Indeed, condom refusal in men has been identified as a health and social crisis beyond Botswana. For example, among young Black men in three cities in the United States, 47 per cent had refused to use a condom at their partner's request in the previous two months (Geter and Crosby, 2014). Ultimately, my participants' experiences of men as sexually irresponsible are supported by a wide body of research pointing to a culture of multiple concurrent sexual relationships and intermittent condom use among men, which intersects with chronic paternal absenteeism to contribute to the high incidence of single motherhood.

There was some discrepancy among my participants in terms of whether they viewed the prevalence of paternal absenteeism as a new phenomenon. Some implied that women of their grandmothers' generation could rely on the economic protection they received from male breadwinners in ways that women of younger generations could not. However, men have historically resided separately from their nuclear families, since cattle posts in isolated areas took them away from their home villages for much of the year (Townsend, 1997). More recently, the creation of new employment opportunities for men in the mines and farms of South Africa led to mass labour migration out of Botswana from the 1940s. By 1943, 10 per cent of the population were absent labour migrants, a number that increased rapidly in the following years (Brown, 1983). Internal migration largely replaced external migration with the establishment of an independent administration in 1966, a time of increased prospects for men within the country following the discovery of valuable metals and minerals (Brown, 1983). Often men were gone for years at a time; money was not always sent home and some men could not be relied upon to return home at all (Brown, 1983). Though male earners were historically separated from their wives and children and were sometimes unreliable, the availability of paid labour was perhaps more consistent in the mining era than it is today. Unemployment for men and women combined has almost doubled since 1991 (World Bank, 2022), a trend that might explain the participants' perception of unreliable male providers as a recent shift.

Nonetheless, other participants asserted that the inconsistency of male familial provision is longstanding. For these women, what was new was that women were able to be self-sufficient in the absence of a male provider in ways that their grandmothers were not, enabling greater autonomy in their life choices. When Pamela found herself in a troubled relationship with her daughter's father she was able to decide, 'I don't need this kind of person in my life' and she 'chose to be a single mother'. Pamela, who was thirty, perceived that had she belonged to an earlier generation she would have feared, 'if I take my child and leave [...] how am I going to survive? How am I going to have food on the table?' She believed that 'in the olden days women were not allowed to do anything, to have a say in how to run their lives', whereas she was able to make choices about her relationship because she knew she could 'afford to do everything that he could do' for her, that she could 'take care of me and my daughter without the help of any man'.

Perceptions of global influence

Many of my participants attributed changes in women's lives to international influences, particularly those permeating from Europe and North America. Schapera (1940: 112–13) commented on 'the growth of new wants' from the late nineteenth century onwards as international trade increased under the British administration, reporting that women 'insist[ed] on having their blankets and dresses', 'young men' had 'acquired tastes in clothing, food and amusement not shared by their elders' and parents wanted to meet their children's demands for 'such extreme local luxuries as bicycles, newspapers and even gramophones'. He revealed that the impact of such 'new commodities, and the creation of wants formerly unknown' was felt in 'greater differentiation in standards of living'. With the novel availability of a wide range of goods, 'new criteria of wealth and social status' had emerged, giving social weight to novel possessions and activities. Schapera's observations hold true today; material desires, and the regret felt when they could not be met, were expressed by several of my participants. Mpho explained that people want 'the house, the private schools'. Since so many women were compelled to survive as single mothers, they frequently had to sacrifice their material aspirations. It could be suggested that the ever-expanding availability of goods and services presented to those with disposable income heightened the loss of male financial support, particularly for women with dependents of their own.

Iversen (2005) suggests that desire for luxuries such as clothing, fine dining, and travel motivates a large number of women to engage in transactional relationships, whereby a series of boyfriends provide funds in return for sexual intercourse. While Iversen (2005) acknowledges that some women control the decision making in such relationships, she points out that gendered social customs and economic inequality create an imbalance of power that usually disadvantages women. Mabedi expressed concern about transactional relationships, which she believed were becoming more common as a result of growing materialism. She contended, 'because of globalization [girls] need to live the fancy life [...] there's a pressure to look good, to show off, and the only way you can get that is from a man [...] because for sure no woman is gonna give it to you'. Her assertion that women will not support one another in achieving material success is perhaps suggestive of competition felt between women, particularly in rural areas where there are few opportunities for women to gain financial independence through employment, and a scarcity of economically established men who could provide for them.

In such a context, women might find themselves competing for resources that could offer means to material satiety. Mabedi, who was twenty-six, said of her peers: 'we sort of emulate what is happening in other countries', girls 'idolize Beyoncé and Kim Kardashian' and the material signifiers of fame and fortune. Pono, who was thirty, had similar concerns about the youngest generation: 'young girls just want to see themselves one day on TV, and that's the lifestyle that they tend to desire more than education and helping themselves grow'. Given that Schapera observed aspirations for European commodities many decades ago, it is striking that the participants complained of external materialistic influences as a recent phenomenon affecting only the youngest generations. In parallel with my participants, Schapera's older interviewees complained that the youth were not only unduly enthralled by alien commodities, but were lacking direction, behaving in an unruly manner and asserting their independence as a result of influences from the Global North. Speaking of the change perceived amid the young, one man told Schapera (1940: 242), 'we never heard of these things until the white man came'. For my participants, it was not the presence of white people that was to blame for the youth losing their way, but the ubiquitous influence of North American celebrity culture.

A minority of the participants spoke about the impact of international influences on women's health. Kesegofetse, a highly educated rural woman, explained that the construction of certain illnesses as 'Western' prevented many uneducated rural women from receiving the treatment they needed. She shared that 'issues like cervical cancer, breast cancer' were thought to impact only white women, and that suggestions to the contrary would be treated with suspicion. Scholars have shown that such a view also affects attitudes towards HIV/AIDS. Though educational programmes and testing clinics are available throughout the country, including in rural areas, the construction of HIV/AIDS as *bolwetse jwa ko toropong* ('an external problem') is persistent (Mathangwane, 2011: 201). Some of those living in villages perceive that HIV/AIDS is not a matter of concern for them, owing to the belief that the disease is an import from the Global North and affects only those living in the metropolitan centres (Mathangwane, 2011). Such an attitude functions as a distancing method; constructing illnesses as foreign reduces the sense of threat a community might otherwise feel, paradoxically increasing the threat by limiting the motivation for prevention, testing and treatment of HIV/AIDS and other potentially fatal diseases (Mathangwane, 2011).

Mabedi, a young rural woman, perceived that 'women empowerment' in Botswana emerged in response to similar movements in neighbouring countries, particularly South Africa. She explained, 'we are watching what is happening to other people and we are doing it also'. Mabedi expressed a view of rural Tswana culture as infertile ground for gender equality, requiring external influences to instigate and sustain changes that empowered women. Such influences were thought to originate from the Global North, establishing new norms in major cosmopolitan cities such as Cape Town and Johannesburg, and ultimately permeating smaller urban locales in the region, including Gaborone. Lesedi, who lived in a village but was working in Gaborone when we spoke, believed that rural women have little choice but to 'rely on that socialization that we grew up with', limiting them to restrictive gender roles. Unlike Mabedi, she thought it unlikely that shifts towards gender equality would take hold in the villages. Lesedi observed that women living in cities had an 'advantage [...] because they can see some things happening differently from typical Tswana culture'. Lenah agreed that in rural areas where 'there isn't a lot of Western influence' women were more likely to be confined by traditional gender expectations. She explained that village women are 'more respectful' towards men, 'will do everything, carry children, bath them, food for the husband', whereas men will be 'at the cattle post or drinking'.

Neo shared that through international travel she had found support in global alternatives to the gender roles available to her at home. She prioritized her education, pursuing a PhD despite pressure from her family to put marriage and childbearing first. While such a path was considered 'unorthodox' and prevented her from feeling she 'fit in', she was able to pursue it with confidence because her international friends were also 'global-minded'. She explained, 'they influence me, making me feel like my decisions are fine'. Neo was able to 'feel normal within [her] group of friends' regardless of challenges from conservative friends and family members back home. Habits she picked up in London, such as drinking 'green smoothies in the morning', doing Pilates and taking up running, caused confusion in her community, where people found her choices strange and unnecessary. She remained unaffected by their concerns and held global influences in a positive light, observing, 'globalization and just the flow of ideas' generated by Batswana students returning from studying abroad were beginning to have a relaxing effect on social norms that was beneficial to women.[4]

Women like Neo selectively practised behaviours and executed decisions according to preferences gleaned from their first-hand experience of local and global lifestyles. While Neo was largely content with her current choices, she was conflicted about her future, struggling to reconcile her career ambitions with her perception of what a family should look like. Neo considered that women's increasing autonomy had negative impacts on family life; as women have 'gotten more opportunities [...] there are a lot of career demands on their time, and I think instead of people spending time with their children and nurturing and growing them, what happens is it's more a material kind of love to make up for the time that you're not there'. Neo was not a mother herself, but she implied that she would prioritize motherhood over her career should she bear children in the future, though she anticipated that motherhood would stall her advancement in her chosen field.

Neo's concern that women's entrance into the labour market is to the detriment of their children is a familiar one, voiced and debated by parents, social commentators, politicians, institutions, scholars and professional experts of all stripes in countries where women have joined the workforce. In 1940 (16) Schapera noted that 'the family in Western society is notoriously being weakened by the emergence of new economic and social forces', and implied that similar shifts were beginning to take place in Botswana at the time. It could be argued that fears of women working outside the home disrupting family life have greater power to limit their career potential in patriarchal, pronatalist societies like Botswana, where constructions of womanhood are confined to the space around childbearing with limited alternatives for social and cultural recognition.

Between two worlds?

As Mpho shared her personal stories with me, she reflected, 'I feel like women right now in Botswana are straddling between this modern and traditional world.' Mpho's framing suggests a view of tradition and modernity as fixed states that cannot be simultaneously inhabited; women are compelled to adapt their behaviours between contexts because they cannot co-exist. Indeed, many of the participants' accounts implied such an interpretation. However, I might suggest that repeated acts of behaviour modification in fact serve to reshape tradition through processes of co-influence and reconfiguration (Jackson et al., 2013), though the emergent ideas and practices may not be evenly or readily applicable in all environments. Connell (2011: 74) acknowledges the possibility of multiple dimensions in the ways gender is structured: it can be 'as if one part of our lives were working on one gender logic, and another part on a different logic'. My interviews provided numerous examples of gender role dissonance and adaptation in the context of existing and emerging cultural and material realities, as I show below.

Women often find the need to balance multiple competing expectations of their conduct stressful and resource intensive. Lesedi's weekly pattern was typical of several of my interviewees: 'I'm working as a teacher, so I come into work to do what is expected from me during the week. But during weekends I be back home in Thama, my home village [...] going to the weddings, going to the funerals.' Funerals occur frequently in Botswana, a tragic consequence of the AIDS epidemic, the leading cause of death in the country (CDC, 2021). Funerals are major affairs typically attended by hundreds of people, all of whom must be fed a complete hot meal. As referred to in earlier chapters, both weddings and funerals demand intensive female labour. The preparation and management of such events was historically a priority for rural women who did not work outside the home and would take up a great deal of their time. However, today many women like Lesedi work formal jobs in the city during the week, travelling to their home villages at weekends to contribute their labour in the community setting. Village communities tend to expect the same level of work from all women regardless of whether they are engaged in employment, and many women must travel long distances to their home villages.

Kesegofetse found the multiple demands on her time and labour to be relentless and exhausting. The labour historically undertaken by women in rural communities was largely physical – ploughing fields, for example. Though modern practices and technologies have displaced much of the need for manual agricultural labour, 'women's work' continues to be primarily physical – cooking, cleaning, carrying and so on. As such, there is limited acknowledgment of the resource-intensive nature of intellectual labour in settlements where such roles are absent or rare. Kesegofetse struggled with her village community's lack of understanding of the work involved in her job as a magistrate. The fatigue she felt at weekends was interpreted as idleness, and her perceived failure to perform the appropriate gender role was met with a punitive response:

> You do live this kind of life from Monday to Friday, then weekends you go to the village, work, you are tired Sunday, you go back to Gaborone, you start working again, you prepare for the weekend. So, probably you'll find that when you get to the village, [...] they will think that you are lazy, when the whole week you have been working in the town and you are very tired. So to them work is physical, physical and not, you know, you can't tell them 'yeah, I am tired' when you are going to offices. Some of them think that I cannot do what other people do, I cannot sweep the yard.

Kesegofetse was seen to fail in the conduct necessary for the 'illusion of gender essentialism' in her community and was socially penalized for it (Butler,

1988: 528). Furthermore, the authority Kesegofetse held as a member of the judiciary challenged the subservience expected of women in her village, which generated tension between her and her neighbours. Kesegofetse's female neighbours were more active than her male neighbours in condemning and excluding her, evidencing the patriarchal bargain – the women of her community perhaps felt threatened by her independence, which undermined a gender regime that offered the security of continuity and other advantages. Kesegofetse persisted in trying to balance her own career aspirations with the gendered expectations of her home community, despite her frustration and the strain on her time and energy. While she was unwilling to sacrifice her career and her independence, being accepted by her community was also a priority.

Malisa experienced similar problems. She lived and worked in a village. Her skilled professional job as a radiographer set her apart from her community, and local women viewed her with suspicion. Consequently she felt unable to connect personally with the women around her. She held them in disdain for what she interpreted as a lack of ambition and an inability to embrace emergent conditions that allowed women to participate in formal employment: 'I regard myself as a modern woman, working-class, but most of my neighbours are just village people who don't even have jobs. [...] I live a totally different life from them. In the morning I just wake up and go to work. Most of them just drink *Chibuku*.'[5] Malisa's professional role in the medical industry bred discord with those in her neighbourhood who were on the whole unemployed. She believed that her community had rejected her because they thought that a woman's place was in the home. With so few options for formal employment in remote areas, particularly for women, Malisa's employed status was something of a local anomaly. Her choices were perhaps perceived as a rejection of prevailing behaviours and attitudes in her village, and as a challenge to the stability wrought by longstanding customs around gender roles. Unlike Kesegofetse, Malisa had given up attempts to win community acceptance through gender-affirming behaviours. She experienced the resulting animosity from her neighbours as mentally fatiguing and expressed frustration at a gender-informed social dynamic she considered to be a no-win situation for her.

Mpho felt obligated to live up to competing expectations:

You have to fill both the professional side of, the, 'okay, she's gone to a good school she has a good job now', you know, 'she can take care of herself and yadda yadda', but on the other side, if you are at a traditional ceremony, 'oh, she can sweep she can cook she can clean, she can work all the domestic duties'.

Mpho felt the weight of expectation to succeed both as an independent, educated and career-driven woman and as a subservient caregiver who is compliant and competent in the domestic sphere. For Mpho, being both willing and able to perform contradictory gender acts was 'what society would judge as successful'. Through the interview process she came to the realization that when she and her mother returned to her grandmother's village, they would both transform 'into that like, perfect daughter and the perfect woman'. She said, 'sometimes I'm even just looking at my mom like, she's you know, she's like, up early, she's sweeping, she doesn't sweep when she's at our house in the city'. Mpho and her mother operated on a context-specific gender logic depending on where they were and who they were with. Mpho shared that her mother, who had a successful international career, nonetheless sought to honour gendered Tswana customs that she felt were meaningful signifiers of her womanhood, such as rising very early to complete household chores. She pressured Mpho to do the same:

I live alone and [my mother] still tells me, 'I know you live alone but you shouldn't be going out and then sleeping in till noon' or whatever. She's like, 'you know you need to get yourself in the habit of being up at six'. I'm like, what am I doing at six!? I live alone, I'm sitting there, it's six o'clock in the morning and I don't know what to do. Yeah but she's like, you know, 'you gotta make your bed and do all of this.'

Though Mpho found her mother's expectations illogical, she did not entirely reject gendered customs. Rather, she selectively participated in the behaviours that worked for her: 'If I'm comfortable with these modern ways I do it, if I'm comfortable with these traditional ways I do it.'

Mpho enacted agency in modifying 'traditional ways' to better suit her lifestyle. For example, by adapting her clothing choices for events that require women to cover their hair and to wear a long skirt or dress rather than trousers: 'I don't think every event I'm at I have to have my hair covered with a scarf.

I can just be like, this scarf doesn't go with my outfit!' She elaborated, 'it's not always practical if you knock off work at five and you have to be there by five thirty, and you're already in pants'. Mpho's career presented practical difficulties in fulfilling customary expectations of her behaviour and appearance, and her keen interest in fashion rendered certain norms of attire unacceptable to her. By acknowledging the constraints of her work schedule and maintaining her personal sense of style, she was able to attend traditionally organized events without compromising her sense of self. While Mpho was reluctant to wear a scarf that didn't match her outfit, she was not hesitant about performing her prescribed duties as a woman of the community, for example, through offering her labour at community events. She was keen to state her appreciation for many Tswana customs, which she felt were an important link to her heritage. For Mpho, adapting rather than rejecting traditional norms was not only a means to social acceptance, but was a way of honouring her cultural identity.

Mpho's modifications were not always deemed acceptable by others and she received criticism for her choices: 'From men and I would say also older women, like for them it's a very fine line. It's like a definite, you do this or you don't do this.' Mpho recalled that at one event: 'One of the [older women] actually said that, you know, "all these young women who are coming, you're coming with pants, you don't have scarfs on your head".' Mpho was frustrated by the older woman's comment, exclaiming: 'I wouldn't have had time to go all the way home to change and then come here!' Though Mpho framed her resistance to traditional standards of attire as a matter of practicality and style, her actions may be interpreted as a meaningful challenge to the sexual objectification manifested in clothing regulation (Whisner, 1982). Clothing choices are trivialized in some parts of the world as superficial (Whisner, 1982), yet, women's ability to determine their personal appearance is significant as an indicator of autonomy in patriarchal societies.

Keeya, who was born and lived in Gaborone, modified her behaviour when she visited rural areas: 'You interact with people differently […] even the way you speak to people at the farm, it's different. […] when I speak to people at the farm my Setswana is more formal. Um, my mannerisms are more formal.' Keeya performed womanhood differently between sites, adjusting the 'bodily gestures, movements, and enactments' that 'constitute the illusion of an abiding gendered self' (Butler, 1988: 519) to fit the localized cultural contexts of city and village. Keeya had not politicized her felt need for such transitions; she did not challenge the requirement for her to alter her conduct in rural settings, nor did she experience it as an unwanted form of social control. By contrast, Shera firmly resisted obligations to act differently in situations that demanded women behave according to gendered customs:

> Researcher: You mentioned a while back that at weekends your mother and your grandmother sometimes have unreasonable demands, what does that mean?
>
> Shera: […] I told [my grandmother] I'm not going to these things anymore […] because all I am is labour. Until I get married I will be labour, and I'm sorry, I'm not fetching tea or fetching things for people, why? What do the men do!? A hundred of them kill one cow. And then they sit. They sit. […] I came back to my mum I'm like, you know, I am not, until you guys renegotiate the policy around labour in this family I will show up when [the men] show up. […] I'm not doing it. I'm not. And they said I was kidding. I am not kidding.

Shera frequently refused to accept gendered demands on her time and labour. Nonetheless, she experienced her resistance as a relentless battle for autonomy: 'it's just constant things like that where you're, either you keep fighting and you say something every single time, which is exhausting and you wouldn't want to do that, or you just keep quiet'. Shera spoke at length about the conflicts she experienced in her continuous struggle for equality with men, many of which I have shared earlier in this book. In a final example, she recalled her astonishment when her partner insisted that if she left their bed unmade 'it takes away from [her] womanhood', an attitude she was completely unwilling to accept. For Shera, reshaping gendered traditions was not an option; she rejected them outright. Her approach was unique among my participants.

Agency and change: An overview

Taken as a whole, my interviews indicated that many women have been impacted by substantial economic, political and systemic change within living memory, and that awareness of such changes is widespread. Some women are able to achieve greater financial autonomy than gendered labour division has historically allowed, though this is somewhat limited to those with access to quality education and to the diverse employment opportunities available in urban centres. Women's presence in government and in the *kgotla* offers representation at the highest levels of decision making that is at least symbolic and may be substantive in some cases. Most of my interviewees indicated that such changes were a break from the past, an observation supported by statistical indicators of reduced gender inequality in these spheres in recent decades. On the other hand, there was little suggestion of meaningful sociocultural shifts in the construction of womanhood and in gender relations at the household and community levels, where gender inequality persists.

A proportion of my participants demonstrated significant agency in their choices, for example, in selecting their careers or in deciding what they would wear. Nonetheless, they were burdened by the felt need to adapt or justify choices, attitudes and behaviours that ran counter to prevailing understandings of women's place in the world. Some women modify even the most persistent traditions to better suit contemporary settings and shape their lives according to their own priorities and preferences. For others, changes in conditions are experienced as stressful as women struggle to balance competing expectations of old and new ways of life. Many felt compelled to behave in specific, culturally determined ways in the presence of men, older women, colleagues, neighbours and other family members, and in some cases friends and partners, to avoid the 'punitive consequences' of failing to perform one's gender appropriately (Butler, 1988: 522). The women in my study who had received minimal education and were living in poor material conditions in rural areas were least likely to give accounts that indicated agency in their choices, though they were largely aware that women in general had more options than they had in the past. Generational differences were also apparent, with participants of all ages observing that social change was most likely to be absorbed and expressed by young women. Such a pattern is typical of ongoing processes of equality, where 'change often starts in one sector of society and takes time to seep through into others' (Connell, 2011: 73).

Notes

1   Future scholarly attention might examine the impact of the colonial administration's Victorian values on gender roles in Botswana, particularly in terms of the Victorian emphasis on gendered labour division and sexual modesty. This chapter is limited to examining the changing role of women as perceived and experienced by my participants; however, a systematic look at patterns, influences and invented traditions over time would firmly situate these changes in their relevant historical context and acknowledge the lasting and widespread impact of colonization on social structures in the country.

2   As noted in earlier chapters, settlement types are not fixed nor their cultural boundaries impermeable; many women distribute their lives between the city and the villages of their kin.

3   The shifting socioeconomic landscape in Botswana was illustrated by the nature of Mosadi Seboko's official inauguration gifts. In place of the customary presentation of cattle, she was given a Toyota truck filled with functional household items, such as a computer and a washing machine (BBC, 2003).

4   The University of Botswana has a well-established Study Abroad Programme, allowing second- and third-year students to study at a partner institution overseas. The programme also allows for inbound international students to study in Botswana.

5   Chibuku is an affordable Sorghum beer that comes in a carton or plastic bottle and is popular in low-income communities across southern Africa.

6

Epilogue

As I wrote this book my thoughts often returned to Joy, the hairdresser I spoke of in the introduction, who talked derisively about men when I met her in Gaborone ahead of beginning my research. Joy's attitude reminded me of Paulina Sebeso, a fictional character in Motswana Bessie Head's 1968 novel, *When Rain Clouds Gather*. Like Joy, Paulina is conscious of women's subjugation under a patriarchal system and resents it deeply. Yet, she is aware that resistance would only bring turbulence to a life already crowded by struggle – it is easier to go along with the myth of male superiority: 'things went along smoothly as long as all the women pretended to be inferior to this spineless species' (Head, 1968/2010: 102). I first read *When Rain Clouds Gather* many years before I began interviewing Batswana women about their lives. The book's damning view of gender relations seemed extreme to me, and I wondered how much of it held true today. Over fifty years after it was written, the women I interviewed paint a picture different only in the details. The modernizing forces that have taken effect since Head's time have changed the socioeconomic landscape of some parts of urban Botswana, bringing new possibilities for a minority of women who have access to the means for independence. Yet, as my research demonstrates, women of various backgrounds remain subject to harmful gendered norms and practices that are rooted in the social and cultural construction of womanhood.

A South African refugee, Head fled to Botswana in 1964 and gained citizenship there in 1979. She claimed that her fiction was apolitical, yet her work frequently related stories of social injustice in Botswana. The female characters in *When Rain Clouds Gather* suffer from severe poverty and the multifarious effects of gender inequality. While Head's work is fiction, the inherent truth in her stories has been widely acknowledged.[1] Writing from the 1960s through the 1980s, Head's novels encapsulate the everyday lives and challenges of Batswana women. Her character Makhaya, a male South African political activist, gives a wrenching commentary on the socialization of Batswana women and the realities of their relationships with men:

> Someone told her that she was inferior in every way to a man, and she had been inferior for so long that even if a door opened somewhere, she could not wear this freedom gracefully. There was no balance between herself and a man. There was nothing but this quiet, contemptuous, know-all silence between herself, the man and his functioning organs. And everyone called this married life...
>
> (Head, 1968/2010: 130–1)

The findings of the present book are consistent with historic studies indicating that women's social status in Botswana is defined largely in relation to men (Schapera, 1938; Schapera, 1940; Suggs, 1987). Only through heterosexual marriage may a woman achieve full participation in adult social life, and childbearing is necessary for recognition as a 'complete' woman in the community. The implications are arguably most damaging for women affected by poverty, women who are unable to conceive and for women in abusive relationships with their partners or spouses. I have demonstrated that the status-conferring nature of marriage and motherhood renders them attractive despite a widely held view of men as irresponsible and unreliable. Many women consider intimate partner violence and unsupported single motherhood to be inevitable, supporting existing data on their prevalence. My research describes a cultural norm in which men are encouraged to have frequent unprotected sex with many different women, yet are not expected to be financially, practically or emotionally responsible for any resulting offspring. Head's Paulina laments: 'Batswana men no longer cared. In fact, a love affair resulting in pregnancy was one sure way of driving a man away, and it was a country of fatherless children' (1968/2010: 133).

In relation to women's labour Paulina reflects, 'no men ever worked harder than Batswana women' (Head, 1968/2010: 117), encapsulating the narrative my interviewees shared in relation to their workloads. This research has shown that women's labour effectively transfers valuable resources, specifically time and money, to men and to married female elders. Multiple factors intersect to generate a disproportionate burden of labour for women as a whole, including the destabilization of historical labour division, increased rates of single motherhood and female-headed households, high unemployment and loss of clearly defined roles among men, women's movement into the market economy and gender roles in the domestic sphere. Further, women take on additional cognitive labour as they navigate and adapt to shifting interests, influences and expectations across different contexts. Women largely experience multiple demands on their resources as overwhelming, unsustainable and unreasonable; they are vulnerable to the detrimental effects of excessive strain on their mental and physical wellbeing and financial stability.

Gender inequality is a resilient and pervasive global phenomenon; women have equal standing with men in just twelve countries (World Bank, 2022a).[2] This book offers a contribution to an emerging body of research addressing the manifestations of gender inequality in contemporary sub-Saharan Africa. According to Connell and Pearse (2015: 83) 'the study of cultural representations of gender, gendered attitudes, value systems and related problems has been probably the most active area of gender studies in the past two decades – in the rich countries of the global metropole. It is not so central in the developing world, where questions of poverty, power and economic change have higher priority.' Indeed, scholarly attention to gender and to womanhood in Botswana over the past twenty years or so has largely focused on the effects of the devastating AIDS epidemic (see, for example: Ho-Foster et al., 2010; Hunter, 2010; Kalichman et al., 2007; Kang'ethe, 2011, 2013 and 2017; Langen, 2007; Letamo, 2003; Mathangwane, 2011; Meekers et al., 2001; Ntseane and Preece, 2007; Phaladze and Tlou, 2006; Phorano et al., 2005; Rakgoasi and Odimegwe, 2013; Seloilwe, 2005; Upton, 2003 and 2010; Upton and Myers Dolan, 2011 and many more).

This important body of research illuminates gendered attitudes and culturally informed social practices from the perspective of HIV/AIDS and its impact on women. My intention is for this book to widen the lens, examining how the social construction of womanhood affects women's lived experience across a range of intersecting issues. A fundamental principle of much feminist research is the desire to draw attention to the voices and beliefs of people who are marginalized. This book brings visibility to the personal experiences and observations of diverse Batswana women, advancing our collective understanding of womanhood in Botswana in a way that is shaped by the values and priorities of the thirty extraordinary women who contributed their stories.

Notes

1   The impact of her writing was officially recognized in 2003, when she was posthumously awarded the *Order of Ikhamanga in Gold* for her 'exceptional contribution to literature and the struggle for social change, freedom and peace' (Government of South Africa, 2003: 20).

2   As measured by indicators in eight key areas: mobility, the workplace, pay, marriage, parenthood, entrepreneurship, assets, and pension. The twelve countries where women and men have equality in these areas are Belgium, Canada, Denmark, France, Greece, Iceland, Ireland, Latvia, Luxembourg, Portugal, Spain, and Sweden (World Bank, 2022a).

Appendix I: Participant information

Table 1 provides information from the demographic questionnaire I asked each participant to complete, and notes whether an interpreter was present at the interview. Contextual details are presented below giving further information, where known, on the participants' place of residence, occupational history, relationship history and status, whether they received any child support and whether they were in contact with their own fathers. Potentially identifying information has been excluded or edited for privacy in cases where participants elected to remain anonymous.

Table 1 Participant Information

Name	Age	Location	Siblings	Relationship	Children	Education	Occupation	Faith	Interpreter
Akhu	39	Urban: Gaborone	Three	Divorced	One	Undergraduate	Musician/Teacher	Christian	No
Basadi	27	Urban: Gaborone	Two	Single	None	Postgraduate	Designer/Researcher	Atheist	No
Beth	33	Rural: Tlokweng	Three	Single	Two	Secondary (partial)	Cashier	Christian	Yes
Elizabeth	34	Rural: Mogoditsane	Six	Married	Three	Secondary (partial)	Driver	Christian	No
Emelda	42	Urban: Gaborone	Seven	Single	Two	Secondary	Self-employed (sales)	Christian	No
Keatlaretse	34	Urban: Gaborone	Six	Single	One	Secondary	Unemployed	Christian	No
Keeya	36	Urban: Gaborone	One	Single	None	Postgraduate	Teacher/Artist	Muslim	No
Kesegofetse	31	Rural: Mochudi	Two	Single	One	Undergraduate	Magistrate	Christian	No
Khana	43	Rural: Mochudi	Five	Single	One	Secondary	Customer Services	Christian	Yes
Laone	35	Rural: Kumakwane	Eight	Single	Five	Secondary	Unemployed	Christian	Yes
Lenah	32	Urban: Gaborone	Five	Married	Three	Postgraduate	Teacher	Christian	No
Lesedi	38	Urban: Gaborone	Four	Single	Two	Postgraduate	Teacher	Christian	No
Maatla	36	Rural: Mmankgodi	Six	Single	One	Secondary (partial)	Unemployed	Christian	Yes
Mabedi	26	Rural: Ramotswa	One	Single	One	Postgraduate	Student	Christian	No
Malisa	43	Rural: Mochudi	Three	Single	One	Secondary	Radiographer	Christian	Partial
Naledi	28	Rural: Ramotswa	Three	Single	One	Secondary	Unemployed	Christian	Yes

Name	Age	Location		Marital status		Education	Occupation	Religion	
Neo	30	Urban: Gaborone	Four	Single	None	Postgraduate	Research fellow	Christian	No
Ona	38	Rural: Kumakwane	One	Single	Two	Secondary (year two)	Unemployed	Christian	Yes
Pamela	30	Urban: Gaborone	Four	Single	One	Undergraduate	Unemployed	Christian	No
Pono	30	Urban: Gaborone	Seven	Married	Two	Undergraduate	Lecturer	Christian	No
Reneilwe	25	Rural: Gabane	Two	Single	None	Secondary	ICT internship	Christian	No
Sefela	45	Rural: Mmankgodi	Five	Single	Three	Primary	Unemployed	Christian	Yes
Shera	34	Urban: Gaborone	Two	Single	None	Postgraduate	Student	Agnostic	No
Taemane	43	Rural: Morwa	Three	Single	None	Primary	Postmaster	Christian	Yes
Mpho	28	Urban: Gaborone	Two	Single	None	Undergraduate	Administrator	Christian	No
Thato	30	Urban: Gaborone	Four	Married	One	Undergraduate	Teacher	Christian	No
Tsala	35	Urban: Gaborone	Seven	Married	Two	Postgraduate	Librarian	Christian	No
Tshepiso	32	Rural: Tlokweng	Two	Single	Two	Secondary (partial)	Cashier	Christian	Yes
Tshiamo	39	Rural: Kumakwane	Three	Single	Two	Secondary	Teacher	Christian	Yes
Tumelo	31	Rural: Mochudi	One	Engaged	One	Undergraduate	Auditor	Christian	No

Akhu

Akhu had lived in Gaborone for most of her life but had spent three years living in South Africa. She was a professional musician and had recently decided to teach part-time to raise the funds for opening her own music school. She had had several boyfriends. The man she married was unfaithful to her while she was away for work, and he filed for divorce soon after her return. She was single at the time of the interview.

Basadi

Basadi attended university in the United States and London. She was pursuing career opportunities in South Africa that allowed her more scope for creativity. Basadi dated a man she met in London for three years, and they remained close after splitting up. She hoped they would rekindle their relationship.

Beth

The father of one of Beth's two children impregnated another woman and abandoned Beth with their newborn infant. It was not clear whether this man was also the father of her oldest child. He did not have any contact with the children and provided no child support.

Elizabeth

Elizabeth and her husband lived together at their home in Mogoditsane, which they shared with Elizabeth's mother-in-law. Elizabeth's husband fathered all three of her children.

Emelda

Emelda lived in Gaborone but was from the village of Ramotswa, where she spent her weekends. She had worked as a poultry farm manager, a hair stylist, a saleswoman and in distribution. Emelda had a child while she was still at school, followed by a second child three years later. The children had different fathers, neither of whom visited their child nor provided financial support.

Keatlaretse

Keatlaretse was living with her mother and sister at their home in Gaborone. She had been working as a secretary but had recently lost her job. She was in a relationship with the father of her son, who abused her emotionally. At the time of the interview, Keatlaretse was waiting for her parents to act on her request to end the relationship. Keatlaretse met her own father for the first time when she was twenty-two.

Keeya

Keeya had grown up in Gaborone and had spent time studying and working overseas before moving back to Gaborone, where she lived alone. She worked as an artist before taking on a teaching role to supplement her income. Keeya had previously been engaged, but her fiancé passed away before they were married. She had recently begun dating again.

Kesegofetse

Kesegofetse formerly worked with the Attorney General in Gaborone, before taking a magistrate position in Mochudi. She hoped to be promoted to judge in the future. Her child's father was not involved in their child's life.

Khana

Khana worked for the Land Board at the time of our interview but in previous years she had supported herself and her daughter by selling goods. Khana had multiple relationships over the years. The relationships ended because the men had sex with other women, drank too much and abused her emotionally. Her daughter's father left two years after she was born and was no longer in their lives.

Laone

Laone hoped to be in a relationship with a kind and trustworthy man, but so far had only dated men who were unfaithful. She offered no information about the father(s) of her children, but she did note that her parents provided for them.

Lenah

Lenah's home village was Serowe and her husband's was Kgalagadi. They visited Serowe and Kgalagadi at weekends to see family and attend events. Lenah had been in teaching since achieving her postgraduate degree in education. She was married, and her three children were all fathered by her husband. She said that her husband was unusual in that he took part in childcare.

Lesedi

Lesedi had two children, the youngest of which (age three) lived with her grandmother. Each child had a different father. The father of the eldest daughter was no longer in their lives. The father of her youngest daughter left Lesedi when she was pregnant and visited the child just once, when she was six months old. He did not contribute financially.

Maatla

Maatla divided her time between her village and a remote cattle post. While she was not formally employed, she was able to support herself and her family through a government poverty eradication programme that provided her with livestock. The father of Maatla's daughter left Maatla when she became pregnant. He did not contribute financially or spend time with his daughter. Maatla was not in contact with her own father.

Mabedi

Mabedi lived between her family home in Ramotswa and her university campus in Kenya. She was in a relationship with a man from Kenya, who was the father of her child. He provided financial support for the family and took care of the child when they were physically together. She was planning to marry her boyfriend the following year, though they were not officially engaged.

Malisa

Malisa had lived in remote parts of Botswana for two years as part of her national service. Her first job was at the local missionary hospital, where she worked as an assistant. After five years in the role, she trained as a radiographer. Malisa was no longer in a relationship with the father of her child. They had a maintenance agreement that he did not honour; however, he provided financial support on a sporadic basis.

Naledi

Naledi had never been employed but hoped to build her own business selling jewellery and clothes or to take a secretarial course. Naledi had a boyfriend, although it was unclear whether he was her child's father. She reported that their relationship was quite good, although he did not allow her to have male friends. She anticipated they would marry soon.

Neo

Neo had studied in South Africa and the United Kingdom. As part of her job Neo worked with institutions such as the World Bank and the Southern African Development Community (SADC). Neo had previously been in a long-term relationship with an English man. Her current boyfriend was a Motswana man and the son of a prominent politician.

Ona

Ona's children were aged ten and fourteen at the time of the interview. They had different fathers, both of whom had lost interest in their children. Ona had requested that each father contribute financially so that she could pay for clothing, food and accommodation, but both had refused.

Pamela

Pamela was from Gaborone and lived there at the time of the interview. She was looking for work when we spoke. If she ran short of money she would buy and sell clothing on the street. Pamela had been in a casual relationship with the father of her child when she fell pregnant. She ended the relationship, and the father did not see the child or provide financial support. Pamela's own father was in prison.

Pono

Pono was raised in the Mahalapye, a town in the Central District of Botswana, and continued to visit her family there at weekends. She studied in South Africa. Pono was previously employed as a quantity surveyor, a job she resigned from when she became pregnant with her youngest child. On the day of our interview, she learned she had secured a new position as a college lecturer. She aspired to run her own business. Pono lived with her husband, who was the father of both of her children. He supported the family financially and assisted with childcare occasionally.

Reneilwe

Reneilwe lived in Gabane at her family home, commuting to Gaborone for work five days a week. She intended to live in Gaborone in the future. She had been with her boyfriend for a year and eight months at the time of the interview. He was ten years older than her. Her previous relationships had been short-lived, and some of her past boyfriends had cheated on her.

Sefela

Sefela had never left her mother's home where she lived with her children, her siblings and her siblings' children. She had struggled at school and had no qualifications, which has made finding employment difficult for her. She hoped to find work that did not require her to read or make calculations. She ran a small tuck store from her yard, selling sweets. The father of Sefela's first child asked her to have a baby. She agreed, but when the child was born he abandoned them.

Shera

Shera was raised in Gaborone but had travelled extensively and was studying overseas. She intended to return to Gaborone upon completing her postgraduate degree. Shera had a long-term boyfriend and described their relationship as complicated.

Taemane

Taemane had lived at her mother's home all her life. For a brief period she had commuted to Gaborone each day to volunteer at a post office, which qualified her for a role at her village post office in spite of her lack of formal education. She had been in relationships in the past, which broke down because the men tried to control her. She had been trying to conceive for most of her adult life and did not know why she had never gotten pregnant.

Mpho

Mpho was born in Gaborone but had spent several years in schools overseas, both in Europe and North America. She lived alone in a house owned by her parents in Gaborone. Mpho spent many weekends visiting family in her parents' home village, Mochudi. Mpho was casually dating at the time of the interview. She had previously had two serious relationships.

Thato

Thato was born and brought up in Gaborone. She had been a contract teacher for several years. She resented not having secured a permanent position. She had originally wished to become a nurse, but her elder sister, who raised her, decided that she ought to teach instead. Thato's husband was the father of her child, and he had been unfaithful to her in the past.

Tsala

Tsala lived and worked in Gaborone, but was born and raised in Mahalapye, where she visited family often. She spent a year studying abroad. She worked as a language teacher for nine years before taking a librarian position at a university. Tsala lived with her husband, who was the father of her children.

Tshepiso

Tshepiso had always lived in the village of Tlokweng. She was not content with her job as a cashier because being on her feet all day tired her and the pay was low. Tshepiso was in a relationship with the father of one of her children. It was unclear whether the father of her first child supported the child financially.

Tshiamo

Tshiamo grew up in the poverty-stricken village of Old Naledi where her grandmother lived, later moving to Kumakwane with her mother and the rest of her family. Tshiamo had worked as a teacher for many years. She also started a tuck shop which her partner ran on a day-to-day basis. Her partner was the father of both of her children. They wished to marry, but her partner could not afford the *lobola* payment. Tshiamo grew up thinking that her mother's husband, who treated the family cruelly, was her biological father. However, she had recently discovered that he was her stepfather.

Tumelo

Tumelo's fiancé was her child's father. Her child was living with his grandmother at the time of the interview, where Tumelo and her fiancé visited him once a month. In her previous relationships she had problems with her boyfriends being unfaithful and exploiting her for money. Tumelo's own father abandoned the family when she started school. She did not hear from him again until she started working. At this stage he contacted her to request financial support, which she provided.

References

Aboderin I (2003) Decline in material family support for older people in urban Ghana, Africa: Understanding processes and causes of change. *Journal of Gerontology* 59(3): 128–37.

Acker J, Barry K and Esseveld J (1983) Objectivity and truth: Problems in doing feminist research. *Women's Studies International Forum* 6: 423–35.

Akinsola HA and Popovich JM (2002) The quality of life of families of female-headed households in Botswana: A secondary analysis of case studies. *Health Care for Women International* 23(6–7): 761–72.

Alcoff L (1987) Justifying feminist social science. *Hypatia* 2(3): 107–20.

Ambert AM, Adler PA and Detzner DF (1995) Understanding and evaluating qualitative research. *Journal of Marriage and the Family* 57(4): 879–93.

Anderson A and Jack DC (1991) Learning to listen: Interview techniques and analysis. In: Berger Gluck S and Patai D (eds) *Women's Words: The Feminist Practice of Oral History*. London: Routledge, 11–26.

Andrews M, Squire C and Tamboukou M (2008) *Doing Narrative Research*. London: SAGE.

Anitha A and Gill A (2009) Coercion, consent and the forced marriage debate in the UK. *Feminist Legal Studies* 17: 165–84.

Babcock Fenerci R and Deprince A (2012) Factors contributing to ongoing intimate partner abuse: Childhood betrayal trauma and dependence on one's partner. *Journal of Interpersonal Violence* 28(7): 1385–402.

Baffour Adjei S (2016) Masculinity and spousal violence: Discursive accounts of husbands who abuse their wives in Ghana. *Journal of Family Violence* 31: 411–22.

Bagai K and Faimau G (2021) Botswana print media and the representation of female victims of intimate partner homicide: A critical discourse analytical approach. *African Journalism Studies* 42(1): 17–35.

Bagwasi MM (2003) The functional distribution of Setswana and English in Botswana. *Language Culture and Curriculum* 16(2): 212–17.

Baltar F and Brunet I (2012) Social research 2.0: Virtual snowball sampling method using Facebook. *Internet Research* 22(1): 57–74.

Bartlett KT (1994) Only girls wear barrettes: Dress and appearance standards, community norms, and workplace equality. *Michigan Law Review* 92(8): 2541–82.

Batsalelwang J and Dambe M (2015) Women's dominance in the informal sector in Gaborone, Botswana. *International Journal of Gender Studies in Developing Societies* 1(1): 25–39.

Bauer G (2010) 'Cows will lead the herd into a precipice': Where are the women MPs in Botswana? *Botswana Notes and Records* 42: 56–70.

Bauer G (2011) Update on the women's movement in Botswana: Have women stopped talking? *African Studies Review* 54(2): 23–46.

Bauer G (2016) 'What is wrong with a woman being chief?' Women chiefs and symbolic and substantive representation in Botswana. *Journal of Asian and African Studies* 51(2): 222–37.

BBC News (2003) Botswana gets first female chief. Available at: http://news.bbc.co.uk/1/hi/world/africa/3194845.stm (accessed 17 August 2022).

Bernick SE (1991) Toward a value-laden theory: Feminism and social science. *Hypatia* 6(2): 118–36.

Bold C (2011) *Using Narrative in Research*. London: SAGE.

Boonzaier F and de la Rey C (2004) Woman abuse: The construction of gender in women and men's narratives of violence. *South African Journal of Psychology* 34(3): 443–63.

Bossuyt S and Van Kenhove P (2018) Assertiveness bias in gender ethics research: Why women deserve the benefit of the doubt. *Journal of Business Ethics* 150: 727–39.

Botswana Press Agency (2017) Teenage pregnancy in schools worrisome. *Botswana Daily News*, 23 March. Available at: https://allafrica.com/stories/201608080713.html (accessed 14 August 2022).

Bourn D (2008) Young people, identity and living in a global society. *Policy and Practice* 7(3): 48–61.

Breen R and Prince Cook L (2005) The persistence of the gendered division of domestic labour. *European Sociological Review* 21(1): 43–57.

Brown BB (1983) The impact of male labour migration on women in Botswana. *African Affairs* 82(328): 367–88.

Browne K (2005) Snowball sampling: Using social networks to research non-heterosexual women. *International Journal of Social Research Methodology* 8(1): 47–60.

Butler J (1988) Performative acts and gender constitution: An essay in phenomenology and feminist theory. *Theatre Journal* 40(4): 519–31.

Campbell DE and Wolbrecht C (2006) See Jane run: Women politicians as role models for adolescents. *Journal of Politics* 68(2): 233–47.

Campbell EK (2003) Attitudes of Botswana citizens toward immigrants: Signs of xenophobia? *International Migration* 41(4): 71–111.

CDC (2021) Global Health Botswana. Available at: https://www.cdc.gov/globalhealth/ countries/botswana/default.htm (accessed 23 August 2022).

Central Statistics Office (2009) *Botswana Demographic Survey 2006*. Gaborone: Central Statistics Office.

Central Statistics Office (2016) Marital status. Available at: https://botswana. opendataforafrica.org/usmspng/marital-status (accessed 28 August 2022).

Central Statistics Office (2018) Botswana Demographic Survey Report 2017. Available at: https://www.statsbots.org.bw/sites/default/files/publications/ Botswana%20Demographic%20Survey%20Report%202017.pdf (accessed 18 August 2022).

Christoforou A (2018) Womanhood, reproduction, and pollution: Greek Cypriot women's accounts of menstruation. *Women's Studies International Forum* 68: 47–54.

Christopher K, England P, Smeeding TM and Ross Phillips K (2002) The gender gap in poverty in modern nations: Single motherhood, the market, and the state. *Sociological Perspectives* 45(3): 219–42.

CIA (2022) CIA World Factbook. Available at: https://www.cia.gov/the-world-factbook/ (accessed 15 August 2022).

Citizenship Rights in Africa Initiative (2022) Botswana: Sithabile P. Mathe and others v. Attorney General. Available at: https://citizenshiprightsafrica.org/botswana-sithabile-p-mathe-others-v-attorney-general/ (accessed 2 September 2022).

Clark S and Hamplová D (2013) Single motherhood and child mortality in sub-Saharan Africa: A life course perspective. *Demography* 50(5): 1521–49.

Closson K, Dietrich JJ, Lachowsky NJ, Nkala B, Palmer A, et al. (2018) Sexual self-efficacy and gender: A review of condom use and sexual negotiation among young men and women in sub-Saharan Africa. *The Journal of Sex Research* 55(4–5): 522–539.

Cole J (2009) Love, money, and economies of intimacy in Tamatave, Madagascar. In: Thomas LM and Cole J (eds) *Love in Africa*. London: University of Chicago Press, 109–34.

Connell R (2005) *Masculinities*, 2nd edition. Cambridge: Polity.

Connell R (2011) *Confronting Equality: Gender, Knowledge and Global Change*. Cambridge: Polity.

Connell R and Pearse R (2015) *Gender in World Perspective*. Cambridge: Polity.

Corbin Dwyer S and Buckle JL (2009) The space between: On being an insider-outsider in qualitative research. *International Journal of Qualitative Methods* 8(1): 54–63.

Cotter A and Savage L (2019) Gender-based violence and unwanted sexual behaviour in Canada, 2018: Initial findings from the survey of safety in public and private spaces. *Juristat: Canadian Centre for Justice Statistics* 1: 3–49.

Creighton MJ, Park H and Teruel GM (2009) The role of migration and single motherhood in upper secondary education in Mexico. *Journal of Marriage and Family* 71(5): 1325–39.

Dados N and Connell R (2012) The Global South. *Contexts* 11(1): n.p. Available at: https://journals.sagepub.com/doi/full/10.1177/1536504212436479 (accessed 21 August 2022).

Datta K (2004) A coming of age? Re-conceptualising gender and development in Urban Botswana. *Journal of Southern African Studies* 30(2): 251–68.

Datta K (2011) 'In the eyes of a child, a father is everything': Changing constructions of fatherhood in urban Botswana. In: Visvanathan N, Duggan L, Wiegersma N and Nisonoff L (eds) *The Women, Gender and Development Reader*, 2nd edition. London: Zed Books, 121–36.

Daymond MJ, Driver D, Meintjies S, Molema L, Musengezi C, et al. (2003) *Women Writing Africa: The Southern Region*. New York: The Feminist Press.

De Beauvoir S (1949/2011) *The Second Sex*. London: Vintage.

Denbow J and Thebe P (2006) *Culture and Customs of Botswana*. London: Greenwood Press.

Deniz P, Lajunen T, Özkan T and Gaygısız E (2021) Masculinity, femininity, and angry drivers: Masculinity and femininity as moderators between driver anger and anger expression style among young drivers. *Accident Analysis and Prevention* 161, article number 10637.

Dintwat KF (2010) Changing family structure in Botswana. *Journal of Comparative Family Studies* 41(3): 281–97.

Dow U (2010) How the global informs the local: The Botswana citizenship case. *Health Care for Women International* 22(4): 319–31.

Eckstein J (2011) Reasons for staying in intimately violent relationships: Comparisons of men and women and messages communicated to self and others. *Journal of Family Violence* 26: 21–30.

Edwards R (1998) A critical examination of the use of interpreters in the qualitative research process. *Journal of Ethnic and Migration Studies* 24(1): 197–208.

Enge M (1985) *Women in Botswana: Dependent yet Independent*. Stockholm: Swedish International Development Agency.

FAO Gender and Land Rights Database (n.d.) Botswana: Other factors influencing gender differentiated land rights. Available at: https://www.fao.org/gender-landrights-database/country-profiles/countries-list/land-tenure-and-related-institutions/other-factors-influencing-gender-differentiated-land-rights/en/?country_iso3=BWA (accessed 12 September 2022).

Finch J (2004) 'It's great to have someone to talk to': Ethics and politics of interviewing women. In: Hammersley M (ed) *Social Research: Philosophy, Politics and Practice*. London: SAGE, 166–80.

Folkvord S, Odegaard OA and Sundby J (2005) Male infertility in Zimbabwe. *Patient Education and Counseling* 59: 239–43.

Fombad CM (2004) The constitutional protection against discrimination in Botswana. *International and Comparative Law Quarterly* 53(1): 139–70.

Friedan B (1995) Beyond gender. *Newsweek Magazine*, 3 September. Available at: http://www.newsweek.com/beyond-gender-182758 (accessed 25 August 2022).

Friedman M (2006) Nancy J. Hirschmann on the social construction of women's freedom. *Hypatia* 21(4): 182–91.

Gaetano A (2014) 'Leftover women': Postponing marriage and renegotiating womanhood in urban China. *Journal of Research in Gender Studies* 4(2): 124–49.

Gage-Brandon AJ and Meekers D (1993) Sex, contraception and childbearing before marriage in sub-Saharan Africa. *International Family Planning Perspectives* 19(1): 14–18+33.

Garenne M, Tollman S, Kahn K, Collins T and Ngwenya S (2001) Understanding marital and premarital fertility in rural South Africa. *Journal of Southern African Studies* 27(2): 277–90.

Gekoski A, Gray JM, Adler JR and Horvath MAH (2017) The prevalence and nature of sexual harassment and assault against women and girls on public transport: An international review. *Journal of Criminological Research, Policy and Practice* 3(1): 3–16.

Gender Links (2022) Botswana: The Constitution – women speak out. Available at: https://genderlinks.org.za/news/botswana-the-constitution-women-speak-out (accessed 2 September 2022).

Gergen KJ (2009) *An Invitation to Social Construction*, 2nd edition. London: SAGE.

Geter A and Crosby R (2014) Condom refusal and young Black men: The influence of pleasure, sexual partners, and friends. *Journal of Urban Health* 91: 541–6.

Gilmore DD (1990) Men and women in southern Spain: 'Domestic power' revisited. *American Anthropologist* 91(4): 953–70.

Government of Botswana (1995) *Policy on Women in Development*. Gaborone: Government Printer.

Government of Botswana (2000) *Botswana Country Report on the Implementation of the SADC Declaration on Gender and Development – The Addendum on the Prevention and Eradication of Violence against Women*. Gaborone: Government Printer.

Government of Botswana (2019) National review for implementation of the Beijing Platform for Action – Beijing+25. Available at: https://www.unwomen.org/sites/default/files/Headquarters/Attachments/Sections/CSW/64/National-reviews/Botswana.pdf (accessed 15 August 2022).

Government of Botswana (2020) Informal sector recovery plan for Botswana 2020. Available at: https://www.undp.org/botswana/publications/informal-sector-recovery-plan-botswana-2020 (accessed 15 August 2022).

Government of Botswana (2021) Press release – adjustment of minimum wages for 2021/2022. Available at: https://twitter.com/bwgovernment/status/1467873329407275010?lang=en-GB (accessed 18 August 2022).

Government of Botswana (n.d.) Background of the judiciary. Available at: https://www.gov.bw/legal/background-judiciary (accessed 15 August 2022).

Government of South Africa (2003) Recipients of the Order Awards 2003. Available at: http://www.gov.za/sites/www.gov.za/files/recipients2003.pdf (accessed 23 August 2022).

Greene CM, Rees S, Likindikoki S, Bonx AG, Joscelyne A, et al. (2019) Developing an integrated intervention to address intimate partner violence and psychological distress in Congolese refugee women in Tanzania. *Conflict and Health* 13: 38.

Harper S and Seekings J (2010) Claims on and obligations to kin in Cape Town, South Africa. *CSSR Research Working Paper* 272. Cape Town Centre for Social Science Research, University of Cape Town.

Harrison A and Montgomery E (2001) Life histories, reproductive histories: Rural South African women's narratives of fertility, reproductive health and illness. *Journal of Southern African Studies* 27(2): 311–28.

Head B (1968/2010) *When Rain Clouds Gather* and *Maru*. London: Virago.

Hesse-Biber SN (2012) Feminist approaches to triangulation: Uncovering subjugated knowledge and fostering social change in mixed methods research. *Journal of Mixed Methods Research* 6(2): 137–46.

Hesse-Biber SN and Leavy L (2007) *Feminist Research Practice: A Primer*. London: SAGE.

Hill C, Miller K, Benson K and Handley G (2016) *Barriers and Bias: The Status of Women in Leadership*. Washington, DC: American Association of University Women (AAUW).

Ho-Foster A, Laetsang D, Masisi M, Anderon M, Tlhoiwe D, et al. (2010) Gender-specific patterns of multiple concurrent sexual partnerships: A national cross sectional survey in Botswana. *AIDS Care* (22)8: 1006–11.

Hobsbawm E and Ranger T (eds) (1983/2015) *The Invention of Tradition*. Cambridge: Cambridge University Press.

Hollos M, Larsen U, Obono O and Whitehouse B (2009) The problem of infertility in high fertility populations: Meanings, consequences and coping mechanisms in two Nigerian communities. *Social Science and Medicine* 68: 2061–8.

Holstein J and Gubrium J (1995) *The Active Interview*. Qualitative Research Methods Series, 37. London: SAGE.

Hunter M (2009) Providing love: Sex and exchange in twentieth-century South Africa. In: Thomas LM and Cole J (eds) *Love in Africa*. London: University of Chicago Press, 135–56.

Hunter M (2010) *Love in the Time of AIDS: Inequality, Gender, and Rights in South Africa*. Indiana: Indiana University Press.

Ibala RM, Seff I and Stark L (2021) Attitudinal acceptance of intimate partner violence and mental health outcomes for female survivors in sub-Saharan Africa. *International Journal of Environmental Research and Public Health* 18(10), article number 5099.

Ingstad B (2004) The value of grandchildren: Changing relations between generations in Botswana. *Africa: Journal of the International African Institute* 74: 62–75.

Iversen AB (2005) Transactional aspects of sexual relations in Francistown, Botswana. *Norwegian Journal of Geography* 59(1): 48–54.

Izzard W (1985) Migrants and mothers: Case-studies from Botswana. *Journal of Southern African Studies* 11(2): 258–80.

Jackson S, Ho PSY and Na JN (2013) Reshaping tradition? Women negotiating the boundaries of tradition and modernity in Hong Kong and British Families. *Sociological Review* 61: 667–87.

Jansen NA and Onge JMS (2015) An internet forum analysis of stigma power perceptions among women seeking fertility treatment in the United States. *Social Science and Medicine* 147: 184–98.

Jewkes R and Morrell R (2010) Gender and sexuality: Emerging perspectives from the heterosexual epidemic in South Africa and implications for HIV risk and prevention. *Journal of International AIDS Society* 13(6): 1–11.

John E (2022) How a new wave of literature is reclaiming spinsterhood. *The New Statesmen*, 16 March. Available at: https://www.newstatesman.com/culture/books/2022/03/how-a-new-wave-of-literature-is-reframing-spinsterhood (accessed 29 July 2022).

Jordan Smith D (2009) Managing men, marriage, and modern love: Women's perspectives on intimacy and male infidelity in southeastern Nigeria. In: Thomas LM and Cole J (eds) *Love in Africa*. London: University of Chicago Press, 157–80.

Kalabamu F (2005) Women's inclusion and exclusion from property ownership in Botswana. In: *6th N-Aerus Conference – Promoting Social Inclusion in Urban Areas: Policies and Practice*. Sweden: Lund, 16–17 September 2005, 1–9.

Kalabamu F (2006) Patriarchy and women's land rights in Botswana. *Land Use Policy* 23: 237–46.

Kalichman SC, Ntseane D, Nthomang K, et al. (2007) Recent multiple sexual partners and HIV transmission risks among people living with HIV/AIDS in Botswana. *Sexually Transmitted Infections* 83(5): 371–5.

Kanda L and Mash R (2018) Reasons for inconsistent condom use by young adults in Mahalapye, Botswana. *African Journal of Primary Health Care and Family Medicine* 10(1): 1–7.

Kandiyoti D (1988) Bargaining with patriarchy. *Gender and Society* 2(3): 274–90.

Kang'ethe SM (2011) Gender discrepancies in the HIV/AIDS community home-based care programme in Kanye, Botswana. *South African Family Practice* 53(5): 463–73.

Kang'ethe SM (2013) Feminisation of poverty in palliative care giving of people living with HIV and AIDS and other debilitating diseases in Botswana. A literature review. *Journal of Virology and Microbiology*, 2013, article number 772210.

Kang'ethe SM (2017) Exploring feminization of HIV/AIDS and Millenium Development Goals (MDG) with examples from Botswana and South Africa. *Journal of Human Ecology* 49(3): 211–17.

Karnieli-Miller O, Strier R and Pessach L (2009) Power relations in qualitative research. *Qualitative Health Research* 19(2): 279–89.

Keetile M and Letamo G (2015) The influences of beliefs and attitudes about antiretroviral treatment on inconsistent condom use in Botswana. *African Population Studies* 29(2): 1749–60.

Kesebonye WM and Amone-P'Olak K (2021) The influence of father involvement during childhood on the emotional well-being of young adult offspring: A cross-sectional survey of students at a university in Botswana. *South African Journal of Psychology* 51(3): 383–95.

Kevane M (2014) *Women and Development in Africa: How Gender Works*. London: Lynne Rienner.

Kinsman M (1983) 'Beasts of burden': The subordination of southern Tswana women, ca. 1800–1840. *Journal of Southern African Studies* 10(1): 39–54.

Klaits F (1997) A research proposal funded by the social science research council: Creating parenthood and childhood in Botswana in the time of AIDS. *Africa Today* 44(3): 327–37.

Kvale S (2006) Dominance through interviews and dialogues. *Qualitative Inquiry* 12(3): 480–500.

La Fontaine J (2003) Professor Isaac Schapera: Anthropologist and champion of the Tswana. *The Independent.* Available at: http://www.independent. co.uk/news/obituaries/professor-isaac-schapera-36716.html (accessed 22 August 2022).

Laing A (2012) Women can inherit the earth rules Botswana judge. *The Telegraph,* 12 October. Available at: http://www.telegraph.co.uk/news/worldnews/ africaandindianocean/botswana/9605346/Women-can-inherit-the-earth-rules-Botswana-judge.html (accessed 15 August 2022).

Langen TT (2007) Gender power imbalance on women's capacity to negotiate self-protection against HIV/AIDS in Botswana and South Africa. *African Health Sciences* 5(3): 188–97.

Legal Information Institute (n.d.) Botswana. Available at: https://www.law.cornell. edu/women-and-justice/location/botswana (accessed 2 September 2022).

LegalWise (2022) LegalWise membership benefits. Available at: http://www.legalwise. co.bw/index.php/products-services/legalwise-membership/ (accessed 19 August 2022).

Lekobane KR (2015) Examining the evidence of the feminization of poverty in Botswana. *Journal of Economics and Behavioural Studies* 7(5): 55–64.

Letamo G (2003) Prevalence of, and factors associated with, HIV/AIDS-related stigma and discriminatory attitudes in Botswana. *Journal of Health, Population and Nutrition* 21(4): 347–57.

Letamo G and Rakgoasi SD (2000) Non-residential unmarried biological fathers and parenting: Child support and father-child contact in Botswana. *Society in Transition* 31(2): 175–83.

LeVine S (1979) *Mothers and Wives.* London: University of Chicago Press.

Magombeyi MT and Odhiambo NM (2017) Poverty dynamics in Botswana: Policies, trends and challenges. *Cogent Social Sciences* 3(1): 1–12.

Mahamid F, Veronese G and Bdier D (2022) Gender-based violence experiences among Palestinian women during the COVID-19 pandemic: Mental health professionals' perceptions and concerns. *Conflict and Health* 16(13): 1–10.

Maharaj P (2001) Male attitudes to family planning in the era of HIV/AIDS: Evidence from KwaZulu-Natal, South Africa. *Journal of Southern African Studies* 27(2): 245–57.

Makgala CJ (2004) A survey of race relations in Botswana, 1800–1966. *Botswana Notes and Records* 36: 11–26.

Makgala CJ and Seabo B (2017) 'Very brave or very foolish'? 'Gallant little' Botswana's defiance of 'Apartheid's golden age', 1966–1980. *The Round Table* 106(3): 303–11.

Makwinja-Morara V (2009) Female dropouts in Botswana junior secondary schools. *Educational Studies* 45(5): 440–62.

Malinga T and Ntshwarang P (2011) Alternative care for children in Botswana: A reality or idealism? *Social Work and Society International Online Journal* 9(2): n.p.

Marandu EE and Chamme MA (2004) Attitudes towards condom use for prevention of HIV infection in Botswana. *Social Behaviour and Personality* 32(5): 491–510.

Marie-Nelly MF (2021) Why we need more girls in Africa in STEM – and how to get them there. Available at: https://www.weforum.org/agenda/2021/04/women-stem-africa-science-gender-education-tech (accessed 9 August 2022).

Mathangwane JT (2011) People's perceptions of HIV/AIDS as portrayed by their labels of the disease: The case of Botswana. *Journal of Social Aspects of HIV/AIDS* 8(4): 197–203.

Mathews S, Jewkes R and Abrahams N (2015) 'So now I'm the man': Intimate partner femicide and its interconnections with expressions of masculinities in South Africa. *British Journal of Criminology* 55: 107–24.

Maundeni T (2002) Wife abuse among a sample of divorced women in Botswana: A research note. *Violence Against Women* 8: 257–74.

Mayer T (1999) Gender ironies of nationalism: Setting the stage. In: Mayer T (ed) *Gender Ironies of Nationalism: Sexing the Nation*. London: Routledge, 1–24.

McAuliffe C, Upshur R, Sellen D and Ruggiero E (2022) You can't report your feelings: The hidden labor of managing threats to safety by women in global public health fieldwork. *PLOS Global Public Health* 2(6), article number e000153.

Meekers D, Ahmed G and Molatlhegi MT (2001) Understanding constraints to adolescent condom procurement: The case of urban Botswana. *AIDS Care* 13(3): 297–302.

Modimakwane DB, Thobega M and Moleele LL (2015) National Education for All (EFA 2015) review report: Botswana. Available at: https://unesdoc.unesco.org/ark:/48223/pf0000231568 (accessed 28 August 2022).

Mogobe DK (2005) Denying and preserving self: Batswana women's experience of infertility. *African Journal of Reproductive Health* 9(2): 26–37.

Mogwe A (1992) Botswana: Abortion 'debate' dynamics. *Agenda* 8(12): 41–3.

Mokomane Z (2005) Cohabitation in Botswana: An alternative or a prelude to marriage? *African Population Studies* 20(1): 19–37.

Molosiwa PP (2016) 'A walking museum of clinical syphilis?' Gender, sexuality, and syphilis in the Eastern Bangwato Reserve, 1930s–1950s. *The International Journal of African Historical Studies* 49(2): 179–94.

Mooko NP (2005) The information behaviours of rural women in Botswana. *Library and Information Science Research* 27: 115–27.

Mookodi G (2004) Male violence against women in Botswana: A discussion of gendered uncertainties in a rapidly changing environment. *African Sociological Review* 8(1): 118–38.

Mookodi G (2008) Gender, policy and family in contemporary Botswana. *Agenda* 22(76): 131–9.

Motzafi-Haller P (2002) *Fragmented Worlds, Coherent Lives: The Politics of Difference in Botswana.* Connecticut: Greenwood.

Mullings B (1999) Insider or outsider, both or neither: Some dilemmas of interviewing in a cross-cultural setting. *Geoforum* 30(4): 337–50.

Mupedziswa R and Ntseane D (2013) The contribution of non-formal social protection to social development in Botswana. *Development Southern Africa* 30(1): 84–97.

Murray CD and Wynne J (2001) Researching community, work and family with an interpreter. *Community, Work and Family* 4(2): 157–71.

Nahar P and Richters A (2011) Suffering of childless women in Bangladesh: The intersection of social identities of gender and class. *Anthropology and Medicine* 18(3): 327–38.

Ngoma Leslie A (2006) *Social Movements and Democracy in Africa: The Impact of Women's Struggle for Equal Rights in Botswana.* London: Routledge.

Ngwako K and Banke-Thomas A (2020) 'I guess we have to treat them, but …': Health care provider perspectives on management of women presenting with unsafe abortion in Botswana. *Global Public Health* 15(9): 1308–21.

Nkomo S and Ngambi H (2009) African women in leadership: Current knowledge and a framework for future studies. *International Journal of African Renaissance Studies – Multi- Inter- and Transdisciplinary* 4(1): 49–68.

Ntoimo LFC and Odimegwu CO (2014) Health effects of single motherhood on children in sub-Saharan Africa: A cross-sectional study. *BMC Public Health* 14, article number: 1145.

Ntseane PG and Preece J (2007) Why HIV/AIDS prevention strategies fail in Botswana: Considering discourses of sexuality. *Development Southern Africa* 22(3): 347–63.

O'Neill ML and Kerig P (2000) Attributions of self-blame and perceived control as moderators of adjustment in battered women. *Journal of Interpersonal Violence* 15(10): 1036–49.

O'Shaughnessy S and Krogman NT (2012) A revolution reconsidered? Examining the practice of qualitative research in feminist scholarship. *Signs* 37(2): 493–520.

Oakley A (1981) Interviewing women: A contradiction in terms. In: Roberts H (ed) *Doing Feminist Research.* London: Routledge and Kegan Paul, 30–61.

Ogundipe R, Woollett N, Ogunbanjo G, Olashore AA and Tshitenge S (2018) Intimate partner violence: The need for an alternative primary preventative approach in Botswana. *African Journal of Primary Health Care and Family Medicine* 10(1): 1–6.

Ortbals CD and Rincker ME (2009) Fieldwork, identities and intersectionality: Negotiating gender, race, class, religion, nationality, and age in the research field abroad. Available at: https://www.cambridge.org/core/journals/ps-political-science-and-politics/article/abs/fieldwork-identities-and-intersectionality-negotiating-gender-race-class-religion-nationality-and-age-in-the-research-field-abroad-editors-introduction/E7B583F128E0B577FFC3C90B61CCC478 (accessed 27 July 2022).

Pansiri ON and Tsayang GT (2017) A situational analysis of basic literacy and numeracy at early grade levels in Botswana. Available at: https://8a02941b-a104-40c9-853d-b99c4c712b1c.filesusr.com/ugd/41ddfd_f74f18553a4b448eb76a1555b388e272.pdf (accessed 18 August 2022).

Park K (2002) Stigma management among the voluntarily childless. *Sociological Perspectives* 45(1): 21–45.

Patai D (1991) US academics and third world women: Is ethical research possible? In: Berger Gluck S and Patai D (eds) *Women's Words: The Feminist Practice of Oral History*. London: Routledge, 137–53.

Patel P (2013) *For women in Botswana, victory against a 'clawback clause'*. Available at: http://www.opensocietyfoundations.org/voices/women-botswana-victory-against-clawback-clause#comments (accessed 7 August 2022).

Peoples FM (2008) Street harassment in Cairo: A symptom of disintegrating social structures. *African Anthropologist* 15(1+2): 1–20.

Phaladze NA and Tlou S (2006) Gender and HIV/AIDS in Botswana: A focus on inequalities and discrimination. *Gender and Development* 14(1): 23–35.

Phillips M (2004) What is tradition when it is not 'invented'? A historiographical introduction. In: Phillips M and Schochet G (eds) *Questions of Tradition*. London: University of Toronto Press, 3–30.

Phoenix A (2010) Suppressing intertextual understandings: Negotiating interviews and analysis. In: Ryan-Flood R and Gill R (eds) *Secrecy and Silence in the Research Process: Feminist Reflections*. London: Routledge, 161–76.

Phorano O, Nthomang K and Ntseane D (2005) Alcohol abuse, gender-based violence and HIV/AIDS in Botswana: Establishing the link based on empirical evidence. *Journal of Social Aspects of HIV/AIDS* 2(1): 188–202.

Pike I, Mojola S and Kabiru CW (2018) Making sense of marriage: Gender and the transition to adulthood in Nairobi, Kenya. *Journal of Marriage and Family* 80(5): 1298–313.

Plummer K (2000) *Documents of Life 2: An Invitation to a Critical Humanism*. London: SAGE.

Procek E (1993) *Changing Roles of Women in Botswana*. Gaborone: The Botswana Society.

Putsch RW (1985) Cross-cultural communication: The special case of interpreters in health care. *Journal of the American Medical Association* 254(23): 3344–8.

Quansah EK (2005) Abolition of marital power in Botswana: A new dimension in marital relationship? *University of Botswana Law Journal* 1: 5–27.

Qunta CN (1987) *Women in Southern Africa*. London: Allison and Busby.

Rabie S, Skeen S and Tomlinson M (2020) Fatherhood and early childhood development: Perspectives from sub-Saharan Africa. In: Fitzgerald HE, Von Klitzing K, Cabrera NJ, Scarano de Mendonça J and Skjøthaug T (eds) *Handbook of Fathers and Child Development: Prenatal to Preschool*. Cham: Springer, 459–71.

Rakgoasi SD and Odimegwu C (2013) 'Women get infected but men die … !' Narratives on men, masculinities and HIV/AIDS in Botswana. *International Journal of Men's Health* 12(2): 166–82.

Ramabu N (2020) The extent of child sexual abuse in Botswana: Hidden in plain sight. *Heliyon* 6(4), article number e03815.

Ranger T (1983/2015) The invention of tradition in Colonial Africa. In: Hobsbawm E and Ranger T (eds) *The Invention of Tradition*. Cambridge: Cambridge University Press, 211–62.

Rapoo C (2013) Constructions of traditional womanhood in Botswana myths and popular culture. *Pula: Botswana Journal of African Studies* 27(1): 5–25.

Raymo JM (2016) Single motherhood and children's health and school performance in Japan. *Marriage and Family Review* 52(1–2): 64–88.

Reich CM, Jones JM, Woodward MJ, et al. (2014) Does self-blame moderate psychological adjustment following intimate partner violence? *Journal of Interpersonal Violence* 30(9): 1493–510.

Ridgeway CL (2011) *Framed by Gender: How Gender Inequality Persists in the Modern World*. New York: Oxford University Press.

Rogers SC (1975) Female forms of power and the myth of male dominance: A model of female/male interaction in peasant society. *American Ethnologist* 2(4): 727–56.

Rudwick S and Posel D (2015) Zulu bridewealth (*ilobolo*) and womanhood in South Africa. *Social Dynamics* 41(2): 289–306.

Ryan-Flood R and Gill R (2010) Introduction. In: Ryan-Flood R and Gill R (eds) *Secrecy and Silence in the Research Process: Feminist Reflections*. London: Routledge, 1–12.

Ryen A (2003) Cross-cultural interviewing. In: Holstein J and Gubrium J (eds) *Inside Interviewing: New Lenses, New Concerns*. London: SAGE, 429–48.

Sardinha L, Maheu-Giroux M, Stöckl H, Meyer SR and García-Morena C (2022) Global, regional, and national prevalence estimates of physical or sexual, or both, intimate partner violence against women in 2018. *The Lancet* 399(10327): 803–13.

Schapera I (1938) *A Handbook of Tswana Law and Custom*. Münster-Hamburg: LIT Verlag.

Schapera I (1940) *Married Life in an African Tribe*. Middlesex: Penguin.

Scharff C (2010) Silencing differences: The 'unspoken' dimensions of 'speaking for others'. In Ryan-Flood R and Gill R (eds) *Secrecy and Silence in the Research Process: Feminist Reflections*. London: Routledge, 83–95.

Schippers M (2007) Recovering the feminine other: Masculinity, femininity, and gender hegemony. *Theory and Society* 36(1): 85–102.

Seloilwe ES (2005) Factors that influence the spread of HIV/AIDS among students of the University of Botswana. *Journal of the Association of Nurses in AIDS Care* 16(3): 3–10.

Sennott, C and Mojola SA (2017) 'Behaving well': The transition to respectable womanhood in rural South Africa'. *Culture, Health and Sexuality* 19(7): 781–95.

Sennott C, Madhavan S and Nam Y (2021) Modernizing marriage: Balancing the benefits and liabilities of bridewealth in rural South Africa. *Qualitative Sociology* 44: 55–75.

Sharp G and Kremer EC (2006) The safety dance: Confronting harassment, intimidation, and violence in the field. *Sociological Methodology* 36(1): 317–27.

Shostak M (1990) *Nisa: The Life and Words of a !Kung Woman*, 2nd edition. London: Earthscan Publications Ltd.

Shu X, Zhu Y and Zhang Z (2012) Patriarchy, resources, and specialization: Martial decision-making power in urban China. *Journal of Family Issues* 34(7): 995–17.

Silberschmidt M (2001) Disempowerment of men in rural and urban east Africa: Implications for male identity and sexual behavior. *World Development* 29(4): 657–71.

Siphambe HK (2000) Rates of return to education in Botswana. *Economics of Education Review* (19): 291–300.

Siphambe HK (2007) *Growth and Employment Dynamics in Botswana: A Case Study of Policy Coherence*. Geneva: International Labour Office, Policy Integration and Statistics Department.

Smith SS (2013) The challenges of procuring safe abortion care in Botswana. *African Journal of Reproductive Health* 18(1): 165–77.

Solway J (2016) 'Slow marriage', 'fast bogadi': Change and continuity in marriage in Botswana. *Anthropology Southern Africa* 39(4): 309–22.

Spivak GC (1988) Can the Subaltern speak? In: Nelson C and Grossberg L (eds) *Marxism and the Interpretation of Culture*. Urbana: University of Illinois Press, 271–313.

Stacey J (1991) Can there be a feminist ethnography? In Berger Gluck S and Patai D (eds) *Women's Words: The Feminist Practice of Oral History*. London: Routledge, 111–19.

Statistics Botswana (2014) Vital Statistics Report 2011. Available at: https://www.statsbots.org.bw/sites/default/files/publications/Vital%20%20Statistics%20Report%202011.pdf (accessed 19 August 2022).

Statistics Botswana (2021) Maternal Mortality Ratio 2019. Available at: https://www.statsbots.org.bw/sites/default/files/publications/Botswana%20Maternal%20Mortality%20Ratio%20%202019.pdf (accessed 20 August 2022).

Statistics Botswana (2021) Vital Statistics Report 2019. Available at: https://www.statsbots.org.bw/sites/default/files/publications/Vital%20Statistics%20Report%20 2019.pdf (accessed 19 August 2022).

Stromquist NP (2001) What poverty does to girls' education: The intersection of class, gender and policy in Latin America. *Compare: A Journal of Comparative and International Education* 31(1): 39–56.

Suggs D (1987) Female status and role transition in the Tswana life cycle. *Ethnology* 26(2): 107–20.

Swartz N, Itumeleng O, Danga AM and Tshwene K (2015) Is a husband criminally liable for raping his wife? A comparative analysis. *International Journal of Academic Research and Reflection* 3(3): 8–25.

The Borgen Project (2019) Single motherhood in South Africa. Available at: https://borgenproject.org/single-motherhood-in-south-africa/ (accessed 18 August 2022).

The Borgen Project (2020) Women's rights in Botswana. Available at: https://borgenproject.org/womens-rights-in-botswana/ (accessed 2 September 2022).

Thomas LM (2009) Love, sex, and the modern girl in 1930s South Africa. In: Thomas LM and Cole J (eds) *Love in Africa*. London: University of Chicago Press, 31–57.

Thomas LM and Cole J (2009) Thinking through love in Africa. In: Thomas LM and Cole J (eds) *Love in Africa*. London: University of Chicago Press, 1–30.

Thupayagale-Tshweneagae G, Mgutshini T and Nkosi ZZ (2012) Where is my Daddy? An exploration of the impact of absentee fathers on the lives of young people in Botswana. *Africa Development* 37(3): 115–26.

Townsend NW (1997) Men, migration, and households in Botswana: An exploration of connections over time and space. *Journal of Southern African Studies* 23(3): 405–20.

Trivedi S and Bose K (2018) Fatherhood and roles of father in children's upbringing in Botswana: Father's perspectives. *Journal of Family Studies* 26(4): 550–63.

Trudgill P and Hannah J (2008/2013) *International English: A Guide to the Varieties of Standard English*, 5th edition. Abingdon: Routledge.

Turnbull B, Graham ML and Taket RA (2016) Social exclusion of Australian childless women in their reproductive years. *Social Inclusion* 4(1): 102–15.

UN (2018) UN Flagship Report on Disability and Sustainable Development Goals. Available at: https://www.un.org/development/desa/disabilities/publication-disability-sdgs.html (accessed 15 August 2022).

UN (2019) Household size and composition 2019: Botswana. Available at: https://population.un.org/Household/index.html#/countries/72 (accessed 24 August 2022).

UN (2021) Drones deliver blood to prevent maternal death in Botswana. Available at: https://news.un.org/en/story/2021/05/1092512 (accessed 1 September 2022).

UN Women (n.d.) Botswana remains committed to the principle of elimination of all forms of discrimination and violence against women (updated). Available at: https://www.unwomen.org/en/get-involved/step-it-up/commitments/botswana (accessed 30 August 2022).

UNAIDS (2022) Botswana 2021. Available at: https://www.unaids.org/en/regionscountries/countries/botswana (accessed 15 August 2022).

UNDP (2012) Gender equality and women's empowerment in public administration: Botswana case study. Available at: https://www.iknowpolitics.org/en/learn/knowledge-resources/case-study/gender-equality-and-womens-empowerment-public-administration (accessed 15 August 2022).

UNESCO (2016) Leaving no one behind: How far on the way to universal primary and secondary education? Available at: http://uis.unesco.org/sites/default/files/documents/fs37-leaving-no-one-behind-how-far-on-the-way-to-universal-primary-and-secondary-education-2016-en.pdf (accessed 18 August 2022).

UNFPA Botswana (n.d.) Gender-based violence. Available at: https://botswana.unfpa.org/en/topics/gender-based-violence-1 (accessed 2 September 2022).

UNICEF (2015) Botswana Annual Report. Available at: https://www.unicef.org/about/annualreport/files/Botswana_2015_COAR.pdf (accessed 15 August 2022).

UNICEF (2019) E Seng Mo Ngwaneng Campaign brief: The National Campaign Against Sexual Exploitation and Abuse of Children. Available at: https://www.unicef.org/botswana/reports/e-seng-mo-ngwaneng-campaign-brief (accessed 31 July 2022).

UNICEF (2020) Education. Available at: https://www.unicef.org/botswana/education (accessed 20 August 2022).

UNICEF (n.d.) Botswana: HIV. Available at: https://www.unicef.org/botswana/hiv (accessed 1 September 2022).

Upton LR (2001) 'Infertility makes you invisible': Gender, health and the negotiation of fertility in northern Botswana. *Journal of Southern African Studies* 27(2): 349–62.

Upton RL (2003) 'Women have no tribe': Connecting carework, gender, and migration in an era of HIV/AIDS in Botswana. *Gender and Society* 17(2): 314–22.

Upton RL (2010) 'Fat eggs': Gender and fertility as important factors in HIV/AIDS prevention in Botswana. *Gender and Development* 18(3): 515–24.

Upton RL and Myers Dolan E (2011) Sterility and stigma in an era of HIV/AIDS: Narratives of risk assessment among men and women in Botswana. *African Journal of Reproductive Health* 15(1): 95–102.

Urdang S (2006) The care economy: Gender and the silent AIDS crisis in southern Africa. *Journal of Southern African Studies* 32(1): 165–77.

USAID (2015) Botswana Maternal Mortality Reduction Initiative. Available at: https://pdf.usaid.gov/pdf_docs/PA00TCKG.pdf (accessed 12 September 2022).

Uttal L (1999) Using kin for childcare: Embedment in the socioeconomic networks of extended families. *Journal of Marriage and Family* 61(4): 845–57.

Van Allen J (2001) Women's rights movements as a measure of African democracy. *Journal of Asian and African Studies* 36(1): 39–63.

Van Klaveren M, Tijdens K, Hughie-Williams M and Ramos Martin N (2009) An overview of women's work and employment in Botswana. Decisions for Life MDG3 Project Country Report No. 5. Available at: http://old.adapt.it/adapt-indice-a-z/wp-content/uploads/2014/09/klaveren_-tijdens_-williams_-martin_2009.pdf (accessed 12 September 2022).

van Niekerk TJ and Boonzaier FA (2015) 'You're on the floor, I'm on the roof and I will cover you': Social representations of intimate partner violence in two Cape Town communities' *Papers on Social Representation* 24: 5.1–5.28.

van Niekerk TJ and Boonzaier FA (2016) 'The only solution there is to fight': Discourses of masculinity among South African domestically violent men. *Violence Against Women* 22(3): 271–91.

Vinnicombe S, De Largy C, Tessaro M, Battista V and Anderson D (2021) The Female FTSE Board Report 2021. Available at: https://www.cranfield.ac.uk/femaleftseboardreport (accessed 21 August 2022).

Wade L (2011) Serena Williams' patriarchal bargain. *The Society Pages*. Available at: https://thesocietypages.org/socimages/2011/05/22/women-damned-if-you-do-damned-if-you-dont/ (accessed 2 August 2022).

Walby S (1989) Theorising patriarchy. *Sociology* 23(2): 213–34.

Wallin AM and Ahlström G (2006) Cross-cultural interview studies using interpreters: Systematic literature review. *Journal of Advanced Nursing* 55(6): 723–35.

Weiser SD, Leiter K, Bangsberg DR, et al. (2007) Food insufficiency is associated with high-risk sexual behavior among women in Botswana and Swaziland. *PLoS Medicine* 4(10): 1589–98.

Whisner M (1982) Gender-specific clothing regulation: A study in patriarchy. *Harvard Women's Law Journal* 73: n.p.

Williamson D, Choi J, Charchuk M and Rempel GR (2011) Interpreter-facilitated cross-cultural interviews: A research note. *Qualitative Research* 11(4): 381–94.

World Bank (2010) Fertility decline in Botswana 1980–2006. Available at: https://elibrary.worldbank.org/doi/abs/10.1596/27493 (accessed 17 August 2022).

World Bank (2015) Botswana Poverty Assessment. Available at: https://documents1.worldbank.org/curated/en/351721468184754228/pdf/88473-REVISED-WP-P154659-PUBLIC-Box394819B.pdf (accessed 17 August 2022).

World Bank (2022) World Bank Open Data. Available at: https://data.worldbank.org/ (accessed 20 September 2022).

World Bank (2022a) Women, Business and the Law 2022. Available at: https://wbl.worldbank.org/en/wbl (accessed 4 September 2022).

Yuval-Davis N (1997) *Gender and Nation*. London: SAGE.

Index

www.ingramcontent.com/pod-product-compliance
Lightning Source LLC
Chambersburg PA
CBHW062030270326
41929CB00014B/2381